T0341982

SARAH SHRIMPTON

MODERN CROCHET

CROCHET

— BIBLE —

Over 100 contemporary
crochet techniques
and stitches

DAVID & CHARLES
—PUBLISHING—

www.davidandcharles.com

CONTENTS

INTRODUCTION

This book is all about showcasing modern crochet at its best – a true reflection of what people are making right now. Think of it as the definitive guide to all the crochet techniques and stitches you'll need to know to create stunning, contemporary pieces. We'll cover the basic stitches, of course – these are the building blocks for any project – and demonstrate new variations and techniques that will enable you to create striking, geometric patterns or elaborate, intricate designs. This book also explores how today's yarn is shaping the modern crochet aesthetic. No longer restricted to a bland palette of fibre, today's crocheters can choose from an ever-evolving variety of yarns made from a whole new range of modern materials: recycled and environmentally friendly, plant-based, vegan, hand-spun heritage fleeces and everything in between, from one-of-a-kind small producers to global manufacturers.

Within these pages, you'll find plenty of patterns to get you started; but it doesn't stop there – modern crochet is also about mixing things up. If you like the graph for the corner-to-corner cushion, but don't need another cushion in your life (it happens to us all), then why not use it for a tapestry-style project instead? Want a hat, but don't fancy a cabled version? Then substitute with a different pattern from the Stitch Variations section (bobbles, perhaps?). Yarns can be changed, too, depending on what you're in the mood for – how about crocheting the Ammonite coaster in giant cord and making a rug? It would certainly be a show-stopper...

There are several sections in this book:

+ The first covers everything you'll need to know for getting started, from hooks, tools and yarn choices to reading patterns, grids, charts and symbols.

+ In the Basic Stitches section there are explanations of all those essential, standard stitches and how to make them, step by step – good for new and experienced crocheters alike.

+ The Stitch Variations chapter demonstrates how, with a slight twist, those basic stitches can be transformed into something quite special.

+ The main section of this book, Modern Techniques, is just that – along with accompanying projects. Here, you'll discover how to create stunning pieces, with photos, charts and grids to help you along the way.

+ Finally, you'll find the section on General Techniques useful for the essential finishing touches to complete your beautiful project, plus some extra help to troubleshoot other issues, too.

GETTING STARTED

LET'S LOOK AT HOOKS

The word crochet comes from the French word meaning 'hook', which, after your yarn, is the next most-important piece of your kit. A standard hook is shorter than a knitting needle, as you only work with one stitch on your hook at a time (apart from a few exceptions). It's also shaped with a hook at one end and a flat part (the grip), which is often stamped with the hook size.

Hooks vary in circumference to work with different yarn weights; from the needle-like 2.25mm (US 1/B) used with lace-weight yarn, to the 40mm used with T-shirt yarn or other extreme yarns. Crochet hooks are often made of aluminium or steel, but you can also find soft, ergonomically engineered ones, as well as beautifully crafted bamboo hooks. The larger hooks (12–40mm/ US 16 and above) are usually made from plastic or wood. While some hooks have their size printed in millimetres on the shaft, many have a letter or number.

CHOOSING THE RIGHT HOOK

This is actually very easy. First, the pattern will suggest a hook size to match the yarn specified. Secondly, check the label on the yarn (look for the crossed needles or hook symbol), but remember it's only a starting point for choosing the size; you may prefer working with a slightly smaller or larger hook than stated. The chart (see right) shows the huge range of sizes available, and how those sizes are referred to in metric and imperial measurements, as well as in the US system.

It can be fun to play with the sizing in some patterns; why not take a delicate doily pattern and, instead of using fine-weight cotton, try extreme yarn and an enormous hook? The result could be very interesting. The projects in this book require a variety of hook sizes, so it's worth arming yourself with a good selection.

HOOK SIZE CONVERSION CHART

Note: this is only a guide. Actual sizes can vary by manufacturer.

MM	Imperial	US
2	14	–
2.25	13	1/B
2.5	12	–
2.75	12	2/C
3	11	–
3.25	10	3/D
3.5	9	4/E
3.75	–	5/F
4	8	6/G
4.25	–	–
4.5	7	7
5	6	8/H
5.5	5	9/I
6	4	10/J
6.5	3	10.5/K
7	2	–
8	0	11/L
9	00	13/M/N
10	000	15/N/P
12	0000	16/P/Q
15	–	19/Q
16	–	Q
19	–	35/S
20	–	36
25	–	50/U
40	–	–

TOOLS YOU'LL USE

Every craft needs a toolkit and crochet is no different. Beyond hooks (and yarn, which will be covered next), you'll find a selection of some of the most useful things below.

SCISSORS

It goes without saying that you'll need to cut things when crocheting – yarn, threads, felt or material – and a decent pair of scissors for the task. Keep them sharp to avoid snagging ends when you are cutting your yarn and thread ends.

TAPESTRY/DARNING NEEDLE

When you have completed your beautiful piece of crochet, you'll have yarn ends to deal with. You can do this by simply sewing the tails into your work to hide them (see Troubleshooting: Weaving in Ends). Tapestry needles have a blunt end, which is less likely to split your stitches, and a large eye for the yarn.

STITCH MARKER

When crocheting, you'll often want to identify an important stitch in your work. It might be the first stitch of a round, or a particularly tricky stitch to see. There are many stitch marker designs available, but you can always use a piece of different-coloured yarn – or even a safety pin – and put this on your stitch instead.

ROW COUNTER

This is useful for keeping track of how many rows or rounds you have completed. You can buy a traditional barrel-shaped counter, download an app to your phone, or keep a tally with pen and paper.

SEWING NEEDLE

Usually much finer than a tapestry needle, this is a sharp-ended needle and therefore perfect for attaching things – like ribbons and buttons – to your work. It has a smaller eye, as it is used with sewing cotton or embroidery threads.

THREAD

If you're going to attach embellishments to your crochet, then you'll need some cotton thread. White and black are a staple in my kit, but you'll probably want to add a few others for variety. You may also like to embroider onto your crochet and, if so, get some colourful embroidery threads for your stash, too.

TOY FILLING

When making a plush item, you'll need to stuff it with something soft. Commercially produced toy filling is readily available and will add substance to your toys and cushions, while conforming to all the proper safety guidelines.

SAFETY EYES

Safety eyes are the little plastic eyes used for toys. You can, of course, embroider features onto your wonderful creation, but you may prefer to use safety eyes instead. They are so-called because the shaft is pushed into the crochet and secured at the back with a tight-fitting washer, making them much more difficult to remove.

RUST-PROOF PINS

When crocheting, you'll often pin things in place or together. You will also need to pin out your crochet if you are blocking your work (see Finishing Up: Blocking), The stainless steel (non-rusting) varieties are essential here, as they won't discolour or leave nasty marks.

FELT AND FABRICS, BUTTONS AND RIBBONS

No crafter can ever have enough of these. Don't forget to raid your 'pile of stuff to be thrown out' and cut ribbons from shirts and fabric from dresses. Crafty knick-knacks are in plentiful supply from high-street haberdashers and online, so arm yourself with a treasure trove of pretties.

POMPOM MAKER

This useful little tool does exactly as its name suggests and is available in all manner of sizes to enable you to make some teeny, tiny pompoms or the great, big, fluffy sort. If, however, you're happy using homemade cardboard rings, that's just as good (see General Techniques: Pompoms).

ALL ABOUT YARN

STANDARD YARN

Standard yarn is just that: it's the 'normal' yarn you would choose for crocheting a hat or making a blanket, the stuff found in abundance in any high-street haberdashery – and the backbone of the fibre market. Produced in every colour of the rainbow, choosing a yarn can seem a daunting prospect, but there are really only two things to consider: yarn weight (how thick or thin it is) and fibre (what it's made of).

YARN WEIGHT

Let's start with weight. It won't surprise you to know that yarn comes in a variety of thicknesses, also referred to as weight, with the finest being 1-ply. See below for a few examples.

Chunky/bulky or 12-ply

Worsted weight or 10-ply

Aran weight or 10-ply

Double knit (DK) or 8-ply

Fingering/sock weight or 4-ply

Lace weight or 1-, 2- or 3-ply

READING THE LABEL

When you buy yarn, it is wound into a ball or skein – often 25g, 50g or 100g – and will have a label around it. This will identify the brand, the yarn name and its weight. There will also be details of the fibre content, washing instructions and often a pair of crossed needles, sometimes a crochet hook, with a recommended size. Other numbers indicate the colour and dye lot. Yarn is batch-dyed in lots, so this means that all of one dye lot will be exactly the same shade. Make sure you have enough yarn of the same dye lot to complete your project, especially for large items requiring several balls of yarn.

SUBSTITUTING YARN

Designers will usually suggest a specific yarn for their pattern, however, there are times when you'll want to find an alternative (you may prefer a different brand or the chosen yarn may be discontinued). In this case, you'll need to ensure that your replacement is the same weight and a similar fibre so that your finished crochet piece will be roughly the same size as the pattern states. That said, for some patterns, size or fibre doesn't matter and you can experiment with whatever yarn you please.

MORE YARN TYPES

There are, of course, modern yarns that push the boundaries and challenge our expectations. Contemporary yarns are a thing of pure joy – choose from natural fibres, affordable acrylics, eco-friendly, recycled, hand-dyed one-of-a-kinds, colour-changing, ombré, fluorescent, sparkly... the list, I'm pleased to say, goes on and on.

YARN FIBRE

As yarn varies in weight, so it also differs in content. It can be made entirely of one material, or a combination of many. The main yarn fibre categories are synthetic, animal and plant.

SYNTHETIC FIBRES

Acrylic and polyester yarns are made of man-made fibres. They are strong, easy to care for and inexpensive, so work well for items subject to everyday rough and tumble, such as blankets, throws and cushions. Synthetic fibres are also used to make novelty yarns such as those containing metallic threads, or the extremely fluffy eyelash yarns.

ANIMAL FIBRES

Wool, alpaca, mohair and silk yarns are luxurious, sometimes fluffy and often a bit more pricey. They have insulating properties, meaning that they're ideal for items to keep you toasty-warm in cold weather.

PLANT FIBRES

Cotton, bamboo and linen yarns are all non-allergenic and feel cool due to their absorbent properties, so they are perfect for clothing, toys and baby accessories.

ECO-FRIENDLY FIBRES

With modern consumers interested in global sustainability, eco yarns are increasing in popularity. New manufacturing techniques mean that materials can be easily recycled, and innovations in agriculture produce crops and livestock with a more environmentally friendly footprint. Alongside the potential to harness renewable energy sources for production, modern eco yarns have never been better.

Easy-to-grow, sustainable crops with a low impact on the environment are also gaining momentum with yarn producers. Various plants, such as hemp, flax – used in linen production – and even nettles, are being processed to produce beautiful, eco-friendly fibres. These are a great choice for crocheters who wish to limit their impact on waste and are ideal for making accessories and wearables.

RECYCLED YARN

T-shirt yarn is made of discarded fabric from the fashion industry and is a clever choice for durable homewares and other sturdy projects. Sold in large bobbins, it can be plain or patterned. Depending on the material it originates from, T-shirt yarn varies in both thickness and stretch; some can be ribbon-like, with little stretch, while others can be extremely elastic.

Other yarns can be produced from recycled fibres too, such as cotton, denim or even luxurious wool and cashmere. More unusual recycled materials include banana fibres from sari textile production, salvaged newspapers and even plastic bottles.

HAND-DYED YARN

Recently, small-scale producers making hand-dyed yarns have become big business in the crochet world. Previously coveted mainly by sock knitters, crocheters realised that they were missing out on this wonderful, one-of-a-kind yarn and have embraced it for creating beautiful shawls, wraps and garments – as well as socks, of course. Hand-dyed yarns can be coloured in a variety of ways, using acid or natural plant dyes, and are often a little pricier than their mass-produced cousins. However, this reflects the time-consuming processes carried out, often by a small team or a single dyer.

YARN INNOVATIONS

Aside from natural and eco-friendly yarns, other advances in the manufacturing industry have driven the modern crochet market. This has resulted in a vast variety of textures, weights and styles of yarn being produced, encouraging crocheters to explore totally new techniques and ways of working.

GIANT YARNS

Made from natural or man-made fibres, these yarns allow crocheters to create beautiful blankets and huge, show-stopping masterpieces in just a short time. These enormous yarns are not plied, meaning they have a low twist, and are therefore surprisingly delicate. To work with these Goliaths of the yarn world, crocheters can choose to use enormous hooks or just their fingers.

STUFFED YARN

This is similar to giant yarn because of its size, but its construction is very different. As its name implies, stuffed yarn is a tube of fabric that is filled with polyester fibre. It can be used in the same way as giant yarn and is ideal for large-scale projects and accessories.

PAPER YARN

Created from materials such as raffia and recycled newspapers, paper yarns are a great choice for creating unusual and striking pieces. As these yarns are not normally waterproof or washable, project choices need to be carefully considered. That said, this type of yarn produces texture and interesting finishes that would not be achievable using standard materials.

OMBRÉ AND GRADIENT YARNS

These beauties are often sold in 'cakes' to show off a gradual colour change from a dark to a lighter hue or from one colour to another. Sometimes these are plied from several strands of yarn, where one is changed at a time to create a seamless blend. Until recently, large yarn manufacturers could not produce such yarns, and it was reserved solely for hand-dyers. A slow change in colour works well with crochet stitches, as there is much less risk of unwanted colour-pooling; this is when colours 'clump' together unattractively in a piece of crochet.

COLOUR-POOLING YARNS

From unwanted colour-pooling to the planned variety, these yarns came about by accident. For a long time, multicoloured yarns that changed colour fairly quickly generated beautiful stripes when knitted, but presented a problem for crochet. However, some crocheters discovered that certain yarns with colour changes of an equal length behaved in a different way when a linen stitch pattern was used, creating a stunning, Argyle-pattern effect. Today, yarn companies are manufacturing dedicated colour-pooling yarns especially for crochet.

LIGHT-INFLUENCED YARNS

Glow in the dark, light-sensitive and reflective yarns are not exactly mainstream, but are a great example of how modern yarn technology is evolving. These yarns are treated with a special dye that reacts to light, or they have strands of reflective material running through them. There are all kinds of uses and applications, especially for children, including toys, accessories and funky garments.

READING PATTERNS, CHARTS AND GRIDS

Crochet instructions can be presented in a variety of formats: as a written pattern, a chart of symbols or a grid of squares. Sometimes, it's helpful to have all three. At the beginning of any pattern there is information about the materials required, including yarn brand, colours and amounts, along with the recommended hook size to complete the project. Finished project measurements are detailed, along with the required tension for the piece (see Troubleshooting: Tension and Measuring for Gauge).

READING A PATTERN

Written patterns usually abbreviate crochet terms to make them easier to read. A pattern will list the numbered rows or rounds in order and provide instructions for all the stitches that need to be made, including any repeats.

You'll quickly pick up how to read a pattern if this is unfamiliar to you, and you can always look up new stitches. Below is an example of the abbreviated pattern style you'll find in this book and how to understand it.

Row 1: ch 1 (does not count as a stitch), dc2tog, dc 3, 3dc in next st, dc 1 across, turn.

Row 1: ch 1 [make 1 chain (this does not count as a stitch so do not work into it)], dc2tog [double crochet 2 stitches together], dc 3 [make 3 double crochet stitches, 1 in each of the next 3 stitches], 3dc in next st [make 3 double crochet stitches all into the next stitch – hence written differently to dc 3], dc 1 across [make 1 double crochet in each stitch across the rest of the row to the end], turn [turn your work before starting the next row].

REPEATED STITCHES

A small group of repeating stitches can be written inside a set of round brackets followed by 'around' or 'across' if it is to be repeated to the end of the round or row, or by the specific number of times it is to be repeated. For more complicated repeats, the start is marked with an asterisk and the finish signalled by a phrase, such as 'rep from *'. If the repeat is over a number of rows, the end is also marked by an asterisk and the phrase 'rep from * to *' is used. Whichever is used, simply repeat the stitches as indicated by the pattern.

ABBREVIATIONS

Written patterns usually abbreviate crochet terms to make them easier to read and will often supply a key. You'll soon get used to working from them and below are the main ones you'll find.

back loops only	BLO
back post treble	bptr
chain	ch
chain space	ch-sp
double crochet	dc
double crochet decrease	dc2tog
double treble	dtr
front post treble	fptr
front loops only	FLO
half treble	htr
repeat	rep
right side	RS
skip	sk
slip stitch	sl st
stitches	sts
treble	tr
triple treble	ttr
wrong side	WS

UK OR US CROCHET TERMINOLOGY

Crochet patterns can be written in UK or US terms. This means that some stitches have different names. This book uses UK terms, and the differences are shown here.

UK STITCH	US STITCH
Double crochet (dc)	Single crochet (sc)
Treble (tr)	Double crochet (dc)
Half treble (htr)	Half double crochet (hdc)
Double treble (dtr)	Triple crochet (trc)
Triple treble (ttr)	Double treble (dtr)
Quadruple treble (qtr)	Triple treble crochet (ttr)

CHARTS

Crochet charts are a visual representation of a pattern, where symbols are used to depict the stitches rather than words. Each row or round will often be numbered to show you where to begin and in which direction to work (right). Generally, charts in rows will begin at the bottom, with odd-numbered rows running from right to left and even-numbered rows from left to right.

chain	○	picot	⬤
slip stitch	•	2tr in same stitch	⋎
double crochet	+	3tr group in same stitch	⋓
treble	⊤	4tr shell in same stitch	⋓⋎
half treble	⊤	5tr shell in same stitch	⋟⋎
2dc in same stitch	⋎⋎	7tr shell in same stitch	⋙⋎
dc2tog	⋏⋏	2tr cluster in same stitch	⬯
5tr bobble cluster in same stitch	⬮	3tr cluster in same stitch	⬮
front post treble	⌇	back post treble	⌇
double treble	⊤	triple treble	⊤
popcorn in same stitch	⬮	puff in same stitch	⬭
dtr popcorn in same stitch	⬮	FLO	⌣
Start of row/round	◀	BLO	⌢

AMMONITE COASTER STITCH CHART

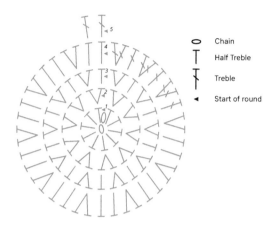

○	Chain
⊤	Half Treble
⊺	Treble
◀	Start of round

GRIDS

Crochet grids can be used instead of, or alongside, written patterns and charts when a complicated colourwork design is better represented as a visual image. Grids are given with tapestry, intarsia, corner-to-corner and filet crochet and show what colours are used for a given stitch in a row – or a block of stitches – and how they sit in relation to each other (below). Some grids only show a small section of a pattern repeat, but read them in the same way as crochet charts, namely from bottom to top, with odd-numbered rows running from right to left and even-numbered rows from left to right, unless the pattern tells you otherwise.

GRID FOR INTARSIA CROCHET BLOCK

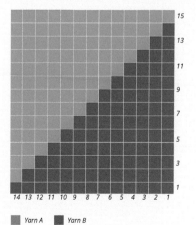

■ Yarn A ■ Yarn B

BASIC STITCHES

All crocheters need to master
the basics, and here you'll find
everything you need to know to
make all of those essential stitches.

ANATOMY OF A STITCH

Tall and short stitches have similar elements, so it's useful to know what's what when it comes to making your stitches. Here we're looking at a sample all in trebles.

'V': once completed, all stitches have a 'V' at their top that points in the opposite direction the stitches are travelling. The 'V' is comprised of two loops, one at the front (facing you) and one at the back. Unless the pattern directs you otherwise, all stitches are made under the 'V' at the top of the stitch.

Post: this is the 'trunk' of the stitch. Essentially, tall stitches have longer posts than shorter ones.

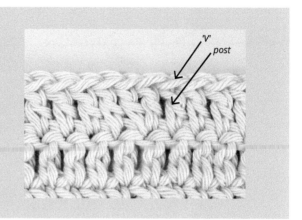

SLIP KNOT

A slip knot forms the very first stitch in most crochet projects. There are several ways to make a slip knot, but this one is the simplest.

1. Make a loop near the end of the yarn ball, leaving a tail. Hold the circle where the strands overlap (A).

2. Using the fingers of your other hand, pull a loop through the circle and place it on the hook. The yarn end can be pulled to tighten the slip knot (B).

CHAIN STITCH (CH)

A chain of stitches is very useful and can be as long or short as required. When working in rows it provides the foundation of your piece, and in decorative work it can produce 3D shapes and interesting spaces.

1. To make a chain stitch, first make a slip knot with the yarn and secure it on your hook (A and B).

2. Twist your hook to wrap the yarn from the **back** over the hook towards the **front**, and under the tip of the hook (this is known as a 'yarn over hook' or just 'yarn over') (C).

3. Catch the yarn with the tip of the hook and draw it through the loop already on your hook to complete the chain stitch (D).

4. Repeat Steps 2 and 3 to make as many chain stitches as needed.

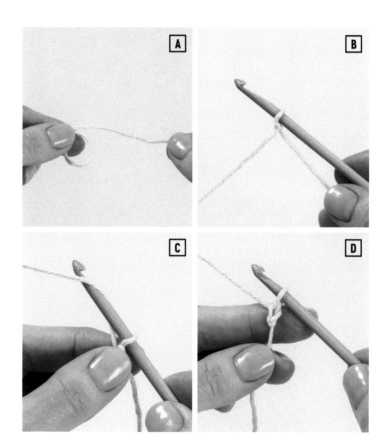

SLIP STITCH (SL ST)

This shallow stitch has almost no height at all and is useful for moving the hook along to a new place or joining stitches together, and it can also be used to create surface detail.

1. To make a slip stitch, insert your hook into the stitch and make a yarn over (E).

2. Draw the yarn through the stitch **and** the loop on your hook to complete the stitch (F).

DOUBLE CROCHET (DC)

US SINGLE CROCHET (SC)

A double crochet is a sturdy, dense stitch, useful for any project where you need the stitches to be close together.

When working in rows, make a turning chain of 1 (see Basic Stitches: Turning/Starting Chains), which doesn't count as a stitch.

1. To make a double crochet, insert your hook into the stitch and make a yarn over (G).

2. Draw the yarn through the stitch (2 loops on hook) (H).

3. Yarn over again (I).

4. Draw the yarn through both loops to complete the stitch (J).

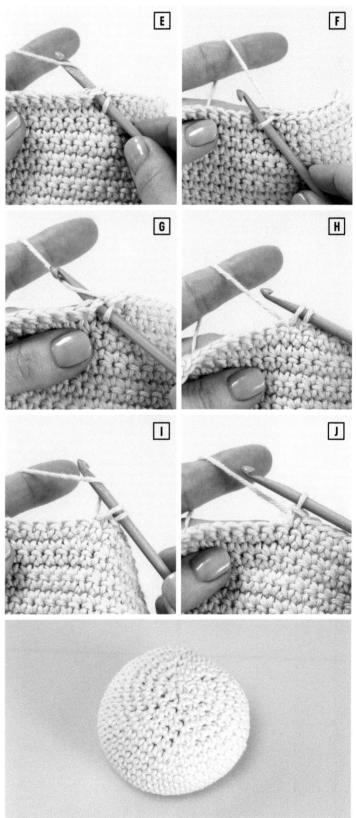

Double crochet is the main stitch used in amigurumi – the Japanese art of crocheting small, stuffed items

TREBLE (TR)

US DOUBLE CROCHET (DC)

A treble stitch differs from a double crochet by being slightly taller. This is achieved by wrapping the yarn around your hook before you begin making the stitch.

Trebles are useful for adding height to your work and are important in making decorative motifs such as granny squares. When working in rows, make a turning chain of 3 (see Basic Stitches: Turning/Starting Chains), which counts as a stitch.

1. To make a treble, yarn over hook, then insert the hook into the stitch (A).

2. Yarn over hook again and draw the new loop through the stitch (3 loops on hook) (B).

3. Yarn over and draw the yarn through the first 2 loops (C).

4. Yarn over and draw the yarn through both loops to complete the stitch (D).

HALF TREBLE (HTR)

US HALF DOUBLE (HDC)

The half treble is exactly that – half of a treble stitch, and its height is halfway between a double and a treble. Like double crochet, the half treble also creates a fairly dense stitch, but with a little more stretch.

When working in rows, make a turning chain of 2 (see Basic Stitches: Turning/Starting Chains), which counts as a stitch.

1. To make a half treble, start with a yarn over hook (E).

2. Insert your hook into the stitch, yarn over hook again and draw the new loop through the stitch (3 loops on hook). Yarn over once more and draw the yarn through all 3 loops to finish the stitch (F).

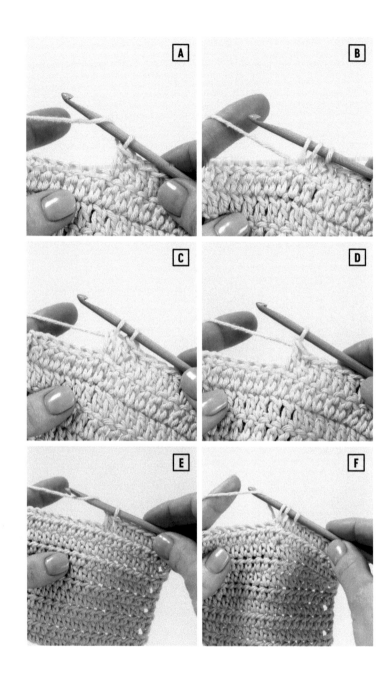

DOUBLE TREBLE (DTR)
US TREBLE CROCHET (TR)
—

This stitch is a taller version of the treble and is perfect for adding height or lacy details to many patterns.

When working in rows, make a turning chain of 4 (see Basic Stitches: Turning/Starting Chains), which counts as a stitch.

1. To make the double treble, wrap the yarn over your hook **twice** (G).

2. Insert the hook into the stitch and yarn over hook again (H).

3. Draw the yarn through the stitch (4 loops on hook) (I).

4. Yarn over again and draw the yarn through the first 2 loops (3 loops on hook) (J).

5. Yarn over and draw the yarn through the next 2 loops (2 loops on hook) (K).

6. Finally, yarn over and draw the yarn through both loops to complete the stitch (L).

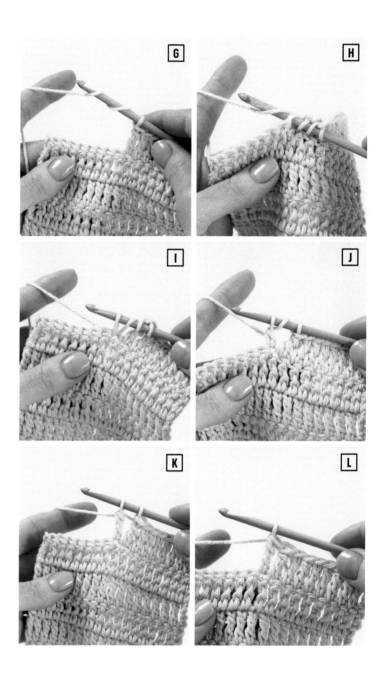

TRIPLE TREBLE (TTR) AND QUADRUPLE TREBLE (QTR)

US DOUBLE TREBLE (DTR) AND TRIPLE TREBLE (TTR)
—

You make these taller stitches by following the same process as the double treble (see previous entry). For the triple treble, wrap the yarn three times over the hook before inserting it into the stitch, and for the quadruple treble, wrap the yarn four times. The stitch is completed in the same way: yarn over and draw the yarn through 2 loops each time, until you have 1 loop left on your hook.

One triple treble

The Mahayana Mandala uses a variety of tall and short stitches singly and in clusters

TURNING/STARTING CHAINS

The turning, or starting, chain at the start of a row or round generally matches the height of the stitches that follow it: a treble crochet pattern will usually begin with a chain of 3, and for anything other than a double crochet, it often counts as a stitch. If you are following a pattern where the starting chain does not count as a stitch, just proceed, working around the chain as instructed.

If, when crocheting you find that your turning chain is too tall and becoming very obvious at the beginning of each row, just crochet a shorter turning chain.

INCREASING STITCHES

To broaden the shaping within a row or round, you need to increase the number of stitches – it couldn't be easier: just add another stitch (or multiple of stitches) into the stitch you are working on. The pattern will tell you exactly how to do this.

2 double crochet (2dc) into same stitch

2 trebles (2tr) into same stitch

DECREASING STITCHES

There are various methods for decreasing the stitch count in a pattern. The simplest way is to skip a stitch or a number of stitches. This leaves a slight gap in the work, which can be used to decorative effect. Often, however, the decrease needs to be less noticeable, and you'll be instructed to crochet 2 or more stitches together.

DOUBLE CROCHET 2 TOGETHER (DC2TOG)
US SINGLE CROCHET 2 TOGETHER (SC2TOG)
—

1. To double crochet 2 stitches together, insert your hook into the first stitch, yarn over and draw the yarn through the stitch (2 loops on hook). Insert your hook into the next stitch, yarn over and draw the yarn through the stitch (3 loops on hook) (A).

2. Yarn over again and draw the yarn through all 3 loops to complete the decrease (B).

TREBLE CROCHET 2 TOGETHER (TR2TOG)
US DOUBLE CROCHET 2 TOGETHER (DC2TOG)
—

1. To crochet 2 treble stitches together, yarn over hook, then insert the hook into the first stitch. Yarn over hook again and draw the yarn through the stitch (3 loops on hook). Yarn over again and draw the yarn through the first 2 loops (2 loops on hook) (C).

2. Yarn over hook, then insert the hook into the next stitch. Yarn over hook again and draw the yarn through the stitch (4 loops on hook) (D).

3. Yarn over again and draw the yarn through the first 2 loops (3 loops on hook) (E).

4. Finally, yarn over and draw the yarn through all 3 loops to complete the stitch (F).

OTHER TREBLE-TOGETHER STITCHES

Sometimes a pattern will ask for several treble stitches to be crocheted together. If this is the case, begin as if you were making a tr2tog and simply repeat from Step 2 for as many stitches as you need.

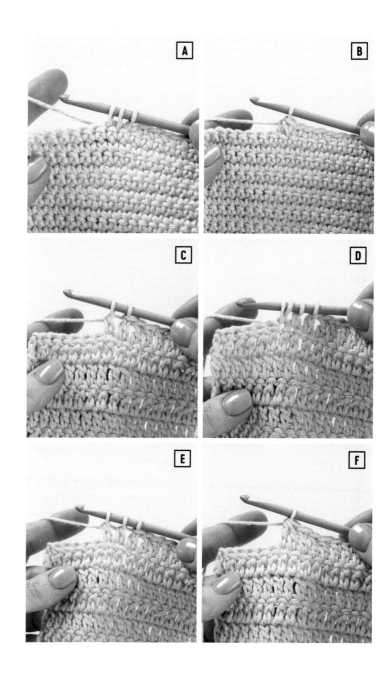

WORKING IN BACK LOOPS ONLY [BLO]/FRONT LOOPS ONLY [FLO]

Where you place your stitches can create interesting effects and textures in your projects, from ribbing and relief patterns to overlay and trellis work. Most often, you will work under the 'V' at the top of the stitch, but there are other things you can try, too.

Back loops only (BLO): make the stitches under the single loop of the 'V' furthest away from you (the back loop).

Front loops only (FLO): make these stitches under the single loop of the 'V' closest to you (the front loop).

WORKING IN BACK POST/FRONT POST

Crocheting around the post of a stitch gives the effect of making the stitch 'pop' forwards or backwards, so it can be used for decorative effects, as well as adding texture. Post stitches can be made with any stitches you like, but it's often the taller stitches that are used – these are much easier to crochet around – as seen here where post stitches are alternated with trebles.

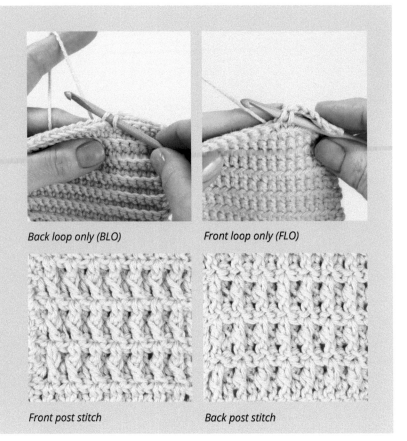

Back loop only (BLO)   *Front loop only (FLO)*

Front post stitch   *Back post stitch*

FRONT POST TREBLE (FPTR)

US FRONT POST DOUBLE CROCHET (FPDC)
—

1. To make a front post treble, yarn over and insert your hook at the **front** and **under** the post of the designated stitch, from right to left, and back out at the front (A).

2. Yarn over and draw the new loop **under** the post of the stitch (3 loops on hook) (B).

3. Now complete the treble in the usual way, yarn over again and draw the yarn through the first 2 loops (C).

4. Yarn over and draw the yarn through both loops to complete the stitch (D).

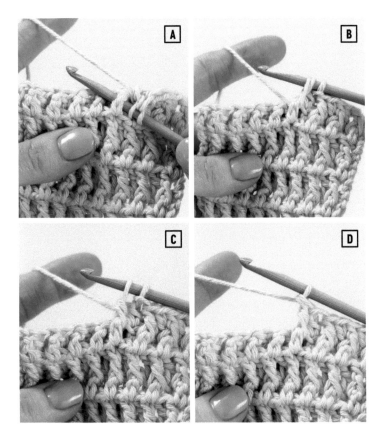

BACK POST TREBLE (BPTR)

US BACK POST DOUBLE CROCHET (BPDC)

—

1. To make a back post treble, you'll work from the back of the fabric: yarn over and insert your hook at the **back** and **under** the designated stitch, from right to left, and bring it out at the back again (E).

2. Yarn over and draw the new loop **under** the post of the stitch (3 loops on hook) (F).

3. Now complete the treble in the usual way, yarn over again and draw the yarn through the first 2 loops (G).

4. Yarn over and draw the yarn through both loops to complete the stitch (H).

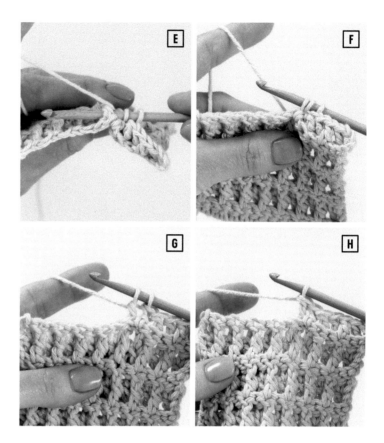

OTHER PLACES TO MAKE STITCHES

Sometimes, a pattern will describe where new stitches are to be placed rather than use an abbreviation – this is often the case for mandalas and other overlay patterns. You might need to make stitches into a chain space or between posts, rather than into the top of a stitch, or it might be that you are asked to work into a stitch several rows below. This is nothing to worry about – simply follow the pattern's instructions that will explain clearly what you need to do.

STITCH VARIATIONS

With a little adjustment, the basic stitches can be combined and transformed into an endless number of new patterns and textures. By just changing where a stitch is placed, or tweaking how it's finished off, you can create incredible new designs. Here are a few that have stood the test of time and are relevant to crocheters of any ability.

UK CROSSED DOUBLE CROCHET
US CROSSED SINGLE CROCHET
—

A simple variant of the standard double crochet stitch (see Basic Stitches: Double Crochet) is just a change to the way the yarn over is worked, which produces these neat little crosses. This method produces a far denser stitch than a standard double crochet, so you might want to increase the hook size. It also works really well in the round, so is perfect for creating homewares with texture or adding interest to your amigurumi project.

1. To make the crossed double crochet, insert your hook into the stitch and take the yarn **under** the hook (A and B).

2. Draw the yarn through the stitch (2 loops on hook) (C).

3. Yarn **under** the hook again and draw the yarn through both loops on your hook to complete the stitch (D).

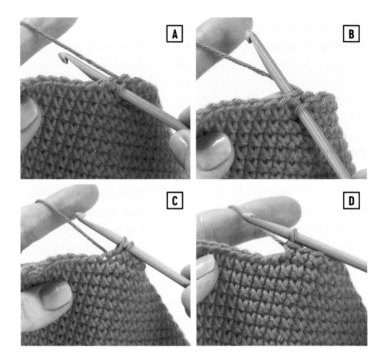

CROSSED CROCHET SAMPLE

Creating the double crochet stitch in this way results in a defined pattern of crosses that stack on top of one another. Many crocheters prefer this method and the effect it produces and use it to replace the regular double crochet stitches in patterns they are following.

UK CENTRE DOUBLE CROCHET (CDC)

US CENTER SINGLE CROCHET (CSC)

—

Centre double crochet, or waistcoat stitch, is another easy variation on double crochet (see Basic Stitches: Double Crochet) and is especially easy to work in the round. You may notice that the finished sample, with its prominent 'V' stitches, produces a knit-like effect. This time, the stitch is made into the centre of the post itself, creating a super-tight stitch with no visible holes at all, so it's suitable for projects like cushions, hats and gloves. Again, you may want to increase your hook size and keep your tension fairly loose, or you'll find it tricky to work your hook into the stitches.

To make the centre double crochet, you'll need to have completed your first round using standard double crochet stitches. For all subsequent rounds, make the stitches in the same way.

1. Insert your hook into the vertical centre of the post under the top loop (the 'V' shape) that is facing you (A).

2. Complete the stitch in the usual way: yarn over hook and draw the yarn through the stitch (2 loops on hook) (B).

3. Yarn over and draw it through both loops (C).

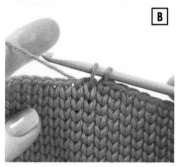

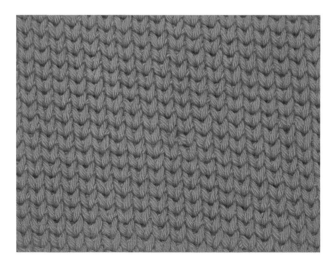

CENTRE CROCHET SAMPLE

The centre double crochet stitches are created by working into the post of a stitch with its right side facing, so this technique is better suited to the projects made in the round (where the right side of the fabric is always facing you). If you want to use this stitch for a project worked in rows, you'll need to join your yarn at the right edge each time, cutting it at the end of every row.

LOOP STITCH

Tactile and eye-catching, this fun stitch is yet another variation on a double crochet (see Basic Stitches: Double Crochet) and is a different way to add texture to projects. As loop stitch can be worked in both rounds or rows, it is pretty versatile, too – great for creating amigurumi sheep or a luxurious, fluffy rug.

1. To make the loop stitch, wrap the working yarn from front to back over the index finger of your left hand, then insert your hook into the stitch. Swing the hook under the yarn behind your finger and grab the yarn with the hook (A).

2. Pull the yarn through the stitch. Adjust the size of the loop (I swap the loop to my right index finger to ensure they are all a consistent size), then yarn over (B and C).

3. Draw the yarn through both loops to complete the stitch (D).

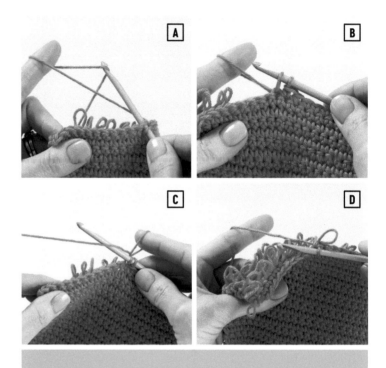

The loops appear at the back of the work so, for them to appear consistently on one side when working in rows, make every alternate row plain double crochet. If you're working in the round, the loops will all be produced on the side away from you. Although this is technically known as the wrong side of your work, the pattern will tell you when to turn this to become the right side. As another variation, you can cut the loops afterwards to create a fur stitch.

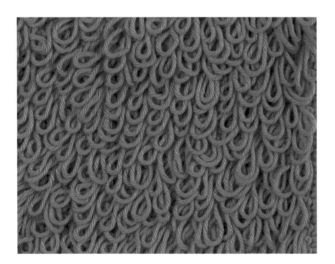

LOOP STITCH SAMPLE

The stitch works with a foundation chain of any length. Make every stitch on an even-numbered row a loop stitch and each stitch on an odd-numbered row standard double crochet.

SPIKE STITCH

A spike stitch is quite simply one that is worked into any row underneath the stitch you would normally crochet into, creating a longer stitch. The length of the spike will vary depending on how many rows you are working over. In the sample, double crochet stitches (see Basic Stitches: Double Crochet) are used, but any stitch can be worked as a spike. This stitch is useful for creating interesting patterns, without the need for frequent colour changes, and is seen in mandalas and other decorative motifs.

1. To make a double crochet spike stitch, insert the hook in the designated row beneath the next stitch (A).

2. Yarn over and draw a long loop of yarn through the stitch, up to the height of the previous stitch (2 loops on hook) (B).

3. Yarn over and pull the yarn through both loops to complete the stitch (C).

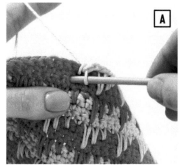

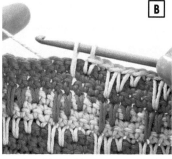

When making the spike stitch, try to keep your tension fairly even: too tight and your work will pucker; too loose and the spikes will lose their crisp appearance.

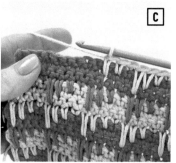

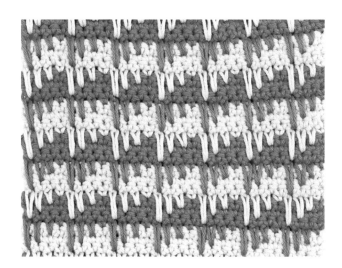

SPIKE STITCH SAMPLE

In the sample, the foundation chain is a multiple of 4, and 4 rows of each colour are made. Make the spike stitches on the first row of a colour change to make them really stand out, with each stitch worked into the next row down over a 4-stitch repeat.

TRADITIONAL BOBBLE STITCH
—

This stitch is made by working 4 or more stitches together – trebles (see Basic Stitches: Treble Crochet) – but this time, all in the same stitch. To make the bobble stand out, the stitches surrounding it are short – often double crochet – but you could use half trebles, if you prefer. The bobble is created on the back of your work, so you'll want to make the alternate rows in a plain stitch.

1. For a bobble with 5 treble stitches, *yarn over hook, then insert the hook into the designated stitch (A).

2. Yarn over hook again and draw the yarn through the stitch. Yarn over again and draw the yarn through the first 2 loops (B).

3. Repeat from * 4 more times (6 loops on hook) (C).

4. Yarn over and draw the yarn through all loops to complete the stitch (D). Sometimes the pattern will ask you to close the bobble with a ch 1.

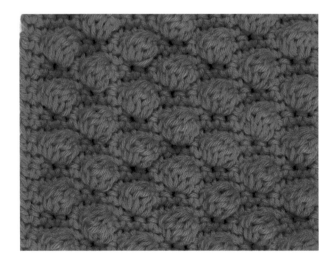

TRADITIONAL BOBBLE SAMPLE

Make your foundation chain a multiple of 6 (minimum of 2 multiples), plus 5 extra chains.

Row 1: ch 1 (does not count as st), dc 1 in each st across, turn.

Row 2: ch 1, dc 1 in same st, dc 4, bobble in next st, *dc 5, bobble in next st; rep from * until 5 sts remaining, dc 5, turn.

Row 3: ch 1, dc 1 in each st across, turn.

Row 4: ch 1, dc 1 in same st, dc 1, bobble in next st, *dc 5, bobble in next st; rep from * until 2 sts remaining, dc 2, turn.

Row 5 onwards: rep **Rows 1–4.**

PUFF STITCH

These mini mounds are created with several half trebles (see Basic Stitches: Half Treble) worked into the same stitch. For a puffier appearance to each one, add more half treble stitches.

1. To make a puff stitch, *yarn over hook, insert it into the stitch, then pull up a long loop (slightly higher than the stitch before) (A).

2. Repeat from * twice more (7 loops on hook) (B).

3. Yarn over and draw the yarn through all loops to complete the stitch (C). Again, the pattern might ask you to close the puff with a ch 1.

Puff stitches are designed to look pretty on the right side of your project, however, they create an interesting pattern on the reverse, too.

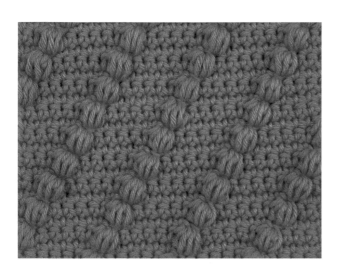

PUFF STITCH SAMPLE

Make your foundation chain a multiple of 5, plus 4 extra chains.

Row 1: ch 1 (does not count as st), dc 1 in each st across, turn.

Row 2: ch 1, dc 1 in same st, dc 3, puff in next st, *dc 4, puff in next st; rep from * until 4 sts remaining, dc 4, turn.

Row 3 onwards: rep **Rows 1 and 2**.

To make diagonal lines of puffs, make the first puff stitch one stitch earlier than the previous puff row, and remember to add a puff after 4 double crochet stitches have been worked at the end of a row.

POPCORN STITCH

Popcorns are multiples of tall stitches worked into one stitch, but closed together at the end. As with bobble stitch, you can use any multiples of the taller stitches to make a popcorn, and likewise you'll want short stitches either side. The beauty of this stitch is that it can pop out on either side of your project, so it can be worked on every row to give a highly clustered finish or to create a double-sided project.

1. To make the popcorn, work 5 treble stitches (see Basic Stitches: Treble) into the designated stitch (A).

2. For a popcorn on the rights side of your work, remove your hook from the working loop and insert it from **front** to **back** through the first treble stitch, and bring your hook round to catch the working loop (B).

3. Pull this loop through the stitch and ch 1 to close the popcorn (C).

4. For a bobble on the wrong side of your work, remove your hook from the working loop and insert it from **back** to **front** through the first treble stitch, and bring your hook round to catch the working loop (D).

5. Pull this loop through the stitch and ch 1 to close the popcorn (E).

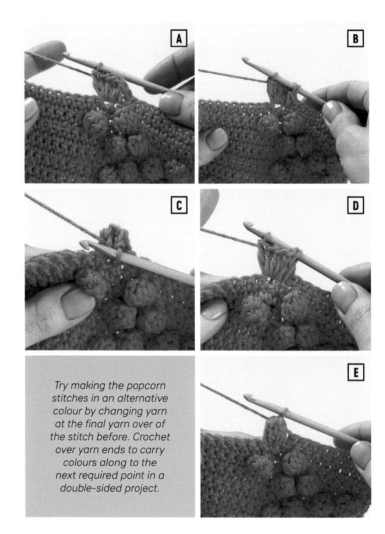

Try making the popcorn stitches in an alternative colour by changing yarn at the final yarn over of the stitch before. Crochet over yarn ends to carry colours along to the next required point in a double-sided project.

POPCORN STITCH SAMPLE

For this sample, there are no rules. Simply make your foundation chain as long as you wish and work the popcorn stitches randomly to create the desired effect. This sample is worked in double crochet.

SHORT STITCH, TALL STITCH

This easy repeat is perfect for adding texture with minimum effort. Short double crochet stitches (see Basic Stitches: Double Crochet) are worked either side of a double treble (see Basic Stitches: Double Treble), causing the taller stitch to bend to the height of its smaller companions. This creates an indentation that pops out on the opposite side.

Make your foundation chain a multiple of 2, plus 1 extra chain.

Row 1: ch 1 (does not count as st), dc 1 in each st across, turn.

Row 2: ch 1, dc 1, *dtr 1 in next st, dc 1 in next st; rep from * across, turn.

Row 3: ch 1, dc 1 in each st across, turn.

Row 4: ch 4 (counts as dtr), *dc 1 in next st, dtr 1 in next st; rep from * across, turn.

Row 5 onwards: rep **Rows 1–4**.

RIPPLE PATTERN

The gentle, wavy rhythm of this ripple pattern, created with decreases and increases, make it ideal for blankets and throws. If you want to change things, try double trebles (see Basic Stitches: Double Treble) and increase the starting chain (see Basic Stitches: Turning/Starting Chains) for the height of stitch, or add more stitches between the increases and decreases.

Make your foundation chain a multiple of 10 (minimum of 2 multiples), plus 1 extra chain.

Row 1: ch 3 (counts as 1tr), tr 1 in 4th ch from hook, tr 3, tr3tog, tr 3, *3tr in next st, tr 3, tr3tog, tr 3; rep from * until one st remaining, 2tr in last st, turn.

Row 2: ch 3 (counts as 1tr), tr 1 in same st as ch3, tr 3, tr3tog, tr 3, *3tr in next st, tr 3, tr3tog, tr 3; rep from * until one st remaining, 2tr in last st, turn.

Row 3 onwards: rep **Row 2**.

CHEVRON PATTERN

Similar to the ripple, but with a more pronounced and spikier cadence, this pattern uses short, double crochet stitches (see Basic Stitches: Double Crochet), this time worked in the back loops only.

Make your foundation chain a multiple of 9 (minimum of 2 multiples), plus 2 extra chains.

Row 1: ch 1 (does not count as a stitch), dc2tog, dc 3, 3dc in next st, dc 3, *sk 2 sts, dc 3, 3dc in next st, dc 3; rep from * until 2 sts remaining, dc2tog, turn.

Row 2 onwards: repeat **Row 1** in BLO.

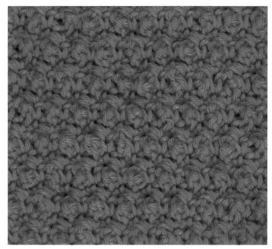

SHORT STITCH, TALL STITCH SAMPLE

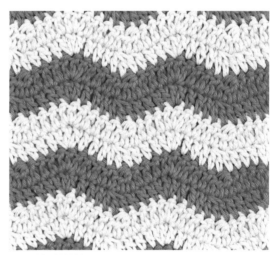

RIPPLE SAMPLE

CHEVRON SAMPLE

MODERN TECHNIQUES

It's interesting how trends come and go, isn't it? Some disappear completely (and for good reason), while others are reworked and transformed into something new. Many of the techniques in this section are based on traditional methods, but revised in an innovative way, using different yarns or altering how or where stitches are made.

CORNER-TO-CORNER CROCHET

Corner-to-corner crochet, or C2C as it's usually called, is a relatively new technique based on various slanting diamond or brick patterns. With C2C, blocks are created from a combination of chain stitches and trebles (see Basic Stitches: Chain Stitch; Treble), making it perfect for projects that need to be square or rectangular. As each block is a square, the C2C technique lends itself perfectly to geometric and pixelated designs. Instead of beginning with a traditional long foundation chain, each block is made individually and worked diagonally, increasing with each row until the halfway point is reached. From here, decreases are made to finish the shaping.

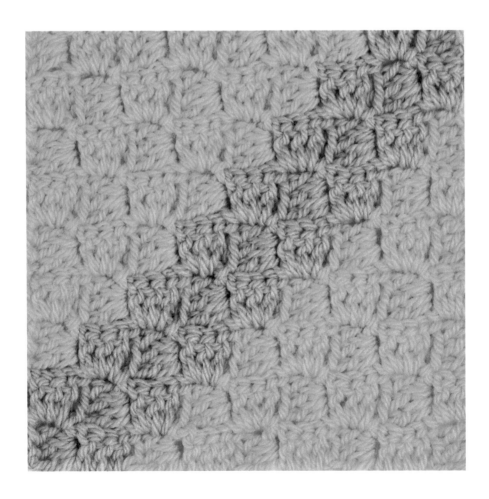

READING A C2C BLOCK CHART

The beauty of C2C is that once you've mastered the row increases and decreases (which are really very easy) you don't need to read a pattern, but can work from a chart instead (see right). Each square represents one block. Begin in the bottom-right corner and work along the rows **diagonally**. Even-numbered rows begin at the bottom edge and then continue up the left side, while odd-numbered rows begin at the bottom-right and continue along the top edge. To keep your place on a chart, you might find it easier to mark off the rows as you progress.

READING A C2C STITCH CHART

Beginning at the bottom-right corner, make the first block (see overleaf) – this is Row 1; then, make the block to its left and work diagonally up to the right to complete Row 2. Row 3 begins directly above, so follow the chart (see below) diagonally downwards to the left. Row 4 starts with the block to the left of the one just completed, and you'll work diagonally up to the right. Continue working in this way until you have completed the chart.

C2C COLOUR BLOCK CHART

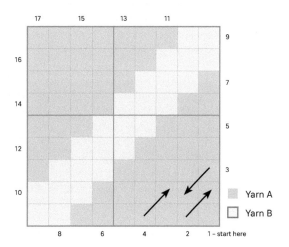

C2C STITCH CHART

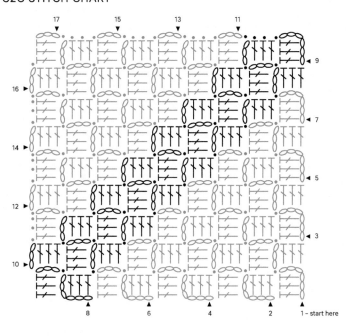

MAKING A C2C BLOCK (INCREASE ROW)

All C2C projects begin with just one block, and you increase by a block at the end of every row. The first row is a single block, and you'll see how the trebles lay at right angles to each other in different blocks.

Row 1: ch 6, tr 1 in 4th ch from hook, tr 1 in each of next 2 ch, turn. (1 block) (A)

Row 2: ch 6 (B), tr 1 in 4th ch from hook, tr 1 in each of next 2 ch (C), sl st into 3ch-sp of adjacent block (D), ch 3, 3tr in 3ch-sp, turn. (2 blocks) (E)

Row 3: ch 6, tr 1 in 4th ch from hook, tr 1 in each of next 2 ch, *sl st into 3ch-sp of adjacent block, ch 3, 3tr in 3ch-sp; rep from * across row, turn. (3 blocks) (F)

Row 4 onwards: rep **Row 3** until the first decrease row.

MAKING A C2C BLOCK (DECREASE ROW)

Next row: one sl st in each of 3 tr just made, ch 3, 3tr in 3ch-sp of block just completed, *sl st into 3ch-sp of adjacent block, ch 3, 3tr in 3ch-sp; rep from * across row (G and H).

Next row onwards: rep previous row, finishing with one block.

Fasten off.

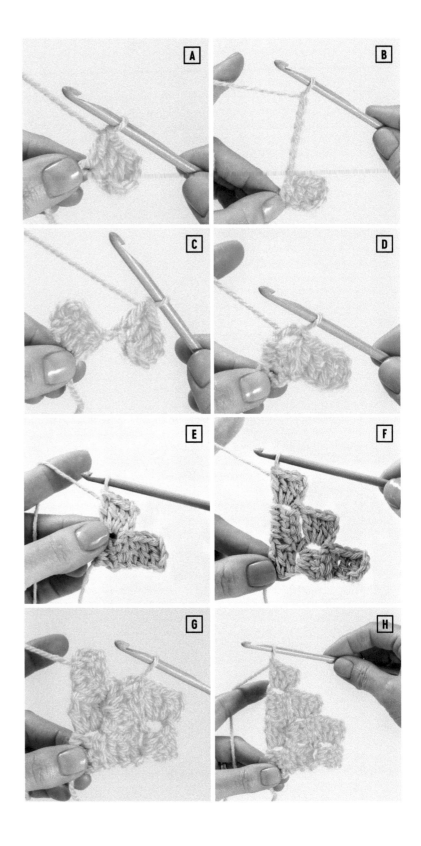

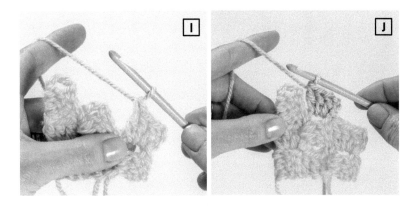

MAKING A COLOUR CHANGE IN C2C

1. When you reach the final treble stitch of the block preceding the start of a different-coloured block, crochet the stitch up to the point of the final yarn over of the last treble. Then, make the final yarn over in the new colour and draw this yarn though the stitch (I).

2. Slip stitch to the next block as usual, and continue with the pattern until the next colour change is required (J).

You may also see the number of blocks to be in each colour written in a pattern as follows:

Row 8: *A: 4, B: 3, A: 4. (11 blocks)*

This indicates that you use Yarn A for 4 blocks, Yarn B for 3 blocks, Yarn A for 4 blocks. This make a total of 11 blocks in Row 8.

LONE STAR CUSHION

Based on quilting motifs from the American Southwest, this bold cushion uses easy treble blocks and C2C crochet with striking results.

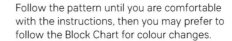

I USED

YARN

Stylecraft Special Aran
(100% Acrylic / 100g / 214yds/196m)

+ Yarn A: White (1001); 1 ball
+ Yarn B: Pomegranate (1083); 1 ball
+ Yarn C: Graphite (1063); 1 ball
+ Yarn D: Aspen (1422); 1 ball
+ Yarn E: Silver (1203); 2 balls

NEEDLES AND ACCESSORIES

+ 5mm hook
+ 40cm (15¾in) square cushion
  insert
+ Tapestry needle

FINISHED SIZE

40 x 40cm (15¾ x 15¾in) square

YOU COULD USE

Any similar Aran or worsted weight
yarn and suitable hook to match
gauge

TENSION

5 x 5 blocks to 10 x 10cm (4 x 4in)
square

Follow the pattern until you are comfortable
with the instructions, then you may prefer to
follow the Block Chart for colour changes.

CHARTED INSTRUCTIONS (MAKE 2)

Follow the chart for the colour changes.

Rows 1–20: increasing.

Rows 21–39: decreasing.

PATTERN (MAKE 2)

Row 1: in E, ch 6, tr 1 in 4th ch from hook, tr 1
in each of next two ch, turn. (1 block)

Row 2: ch 6, tr 1 in 4th ch from hook, tr 1 in
each of next 2 ch, sl st into 3ch-sp of adjacent
block, ch 3, 3tr in 3ch-sp, turn. (2 blocks)

Row 3: ch 6, tr 1 in 4th ch from hook, tr 1
in each of next 2 ch, *sl st into 3ch-sp of
adjacent block, ch 3, 3tr in 3ch-sp; rep from
* across row, turn. (3 blocks)

Rows 4-7: rep **Row 3**. (7 blocks)

Row 8: rep **Row 3**. Change block colours as
follows, E: 1, B: 1, E: 4, B: 1, E: 1. (8 blocks)

Row 9: rep **Row 3**. Change block colours as
follows, E: 2, B: 1, E: 3, B: 1, E: 2. (9 blocks)

Row 10: rep **Row 3**. Change block colours as
follows, E: 2, B: 2, E: 2, B: 2, E: 2. (10 blocks)

Row 11: rep **Row 3**. Change block colours as
follows, E: 3, B: 2, E: 1, B: 2, E: 3. (11 blocks)

LONE STAR C2C BLOCK CHART

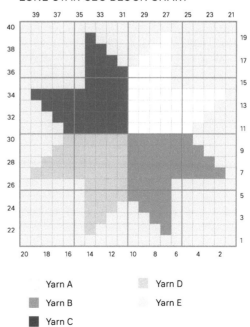

Row 12: rep **Row 3**. Change block colours as follows, E: 3, B: 6, E: 3. (12 blocks)

Row 13: rep **Row 3**. Change block colours as follows, E: 4, B: 5, E: 4. (13 blocks)

Row 14: rep **Row 3**. Change block colours as follows, E: 4, B: 6, E: 4. (14 blocks)

Row 15: rep **Row 3**. Change block colours as follows, E: 1, A: 4, B: 5, D: 4, E: 1. (15 blocks)

Row 16: rep **Row 3**. Change block as follows, E: 2, D: 4, B: 4, A: 4, E: 2. (16 blocks)

Row 17: rep **Row 3**. Change block colours as follows, E: 3, A: 4, B: 3, D: 4, E: 3. (17 blocks)

Row 18: rep **Row 3**. Change block colours as follows, E: 4, D: 4, B: 2, A: 4, E: 4. (18 blocks)

Row 19: rep **Row 3**. Change block colours as follows, E: 5, A: 4, B: 1, D: 4, E: 5. (19 blocks)

Row 20: rep **Row 3**. Change block colours as follows, E: 6, D: 4, A: 4, E: 6. (20 blocks)

Row 21: ch 3, 3tr in 3ch-sp of block just completed, *sl st into 3ch-sp of adjacent block, ch 3, 3tr in 3ch-sp; rep from * across row. Change block colours as follows, E: 5, A: 4, C: 1, D: 4, E: 5, turn, one sl st in each of the 3 tr just made. (19 blocks)

Row 22: rep **Row 21**. Change block colours as follows, E: 4, D: 4, C: 2, A: 4, E: 4. (18 blocks)

Row 23: rep **Row 21**. Change block colours as follows, E: 3, A: 4, C: 3, D: 4, E: 3. (17 blocks)

Row 24: rep **Row 21**. Change block colours as follows, E: 2, D: 4, C: 4, A: 4, E: 2. (16 blocks)

Row 25: rep **Row 21**. Change block colours as follows, E: 1, A: 4, C: 5, D: 4, E: 1. (15 blocks)

Row 26: rep **Row 21**. Change block colours as follows, E: 4, C: 6, E: 4. (14 blocks)

Row 27: rep **Row 21**. Change block colours as follows, E: 4, C: 5, E: 4. (13 blocks)

Row 28: rep **Row 21**. Change block colours as follows, E: 3, C: 6, E: 3. (12 blocks)

Row 29: rep **Row 21**. Change block colours as follows, E: 3, C: 2, E: 1, C: 2, E: 3. (11 blocks)

Row 30: rep **Row 21**. Change block colours as follows, E: 2, C: 2, E: 2, C: 2, E: 2. (10 blocks)

Row 31: rep **Row 21**. Change block colours as follows, E: 2, C: 1, E: 3, C: 1, E: 2. (9 blocks)

Row 32: rep **Row 21**. Change block colours as follows, E: 1, C: 1, E: 4, C: 1, E: 1. (8 blocks)

Rows 33–39: in E, rep **Row 21**.

Fasten off and weave in ends (see Troubleshooting: Weaving in Ends).

TO MAKE UP

Place the pieces with WS facing, and with a slip knot on your hook, work dc 1 into each pair of matching stitches to join the sides around the edge, inserting the cushion pad before closing the last side.

Fasten off and weave in ends (see Troubleshooting: Weaving in Ends).

MOSAIC CROCHET

This is a decorative technique where patterns of geometric shapes and designs are created using a basic combination of stitches. Rows or rounds are worked in alternating stripes of colour, often using double crochet stitches in the back loops only. With mosaic work, the right side needs to be facing at all times, so rows are always worked from the right edge; at the end of every row the yarn should be cut. To create the designs, treble crochet stitches are worked into the unused front loops of stitches two rows below, connecting elements of the design together and creating the mosaic-style patterns.

MOSAIC CROCHET CHART

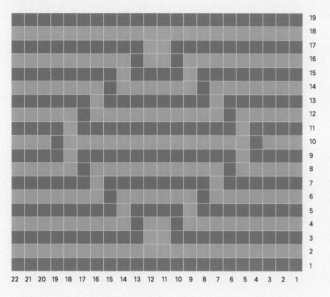

READING A MOSAIC CROCHET CHART

Mosaic crochet patterns use a grid and, unlike standard patterns, need to be read from right to left for **every row**. Although appearing very complicated, mosaic crochet is easy once you understand the basic stitches and techniques of working in the front or back loops only – see Basic Stitches: Working in Back Loops Only/Front Loops Only.

■ Yarn A

■ Yarn B

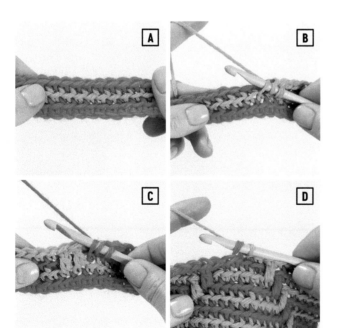

MAKING A MOSAIC CROCHET BLOCK

1. In this sample, the first 3 rows are made by simply working double crochet in the back loops only (BLO) (A).

2. The first element of the pattern begins in Row 4, where stitches 11 and 12 are trebles worked into the front loops only (FLO) of the stitches directly below in Row 2 (B).

3. In Row 5, stitches 10 and 13 are trebles worked into the front loops of the stitches from Row 3 (2 rows below), and so on (C).

4. Once you have crocheted a few rows and have the pattern under way, the rest is easy to follow (D).

RAINBOW WRAP

This wrap uses dark-grey yarn, alternating with a rainbow of colours and a simple mosaic motif to create a fabulous and stylish accessory.

I USED

YARN

Paintbox Wool Mix Aran (50% Wool, 50% Acrylic / 100g / 197yds/180m)

+ Yarn A: Granite Grey (806); 3 balls
+ Yarn B: Tomato Red (812); 1 ball
+ Yarn C: Lipstick Pink (851); 1 ball
+ Yarn D: Blood Orange (819); 1 ball
+ Yarn E: Buttercup Yellow (822); 1 ball
+ Yarn F: Lime Green (828); 1 ball
+ Yarn G: Marine Blue (833); 1 ball
+ Yarn H: Pansy Purple (847); 1 ball

HOOKS AND ACCESSORIES

+ 6mm hook

FINISHED SIZE

140 x 39cm (55 x 15½in)

YOU COULD USE

Any similar Aran or worsted weight yarn and suitable hook to match gauge

TENSION

10 x 10 cm (4 x 4in) square: 14 sts and 14 rows (using 6mm hook measured over pattern)

Leave long yarn tails of 20cm (8in) at the beginning and end of each row. They will be transformed into a design feature as the decorative fringing of your finished project.

This chart shows the repeating section of the Rainbow Wrap, and the pattern states there are 2 extra double crochet stitches at the beginning and end of each row.

RAINBOW WRAP CHART

PATTERN

Begin each row with a standing double crochet stitch (see Troubleshooting: Standing Stitch). All double crochet stitches to be made in BLO. All trebles to be made in unused FLO of stitch 2 rows directly below. Do not turn work.

In A, using chainless double crochet foundation method (see Troubleshooting: Chainless Foundation Stitch), make 202 sts; or, ch 203, starting in 2nd ch from hook, dc 202.

Row 1: dc 1 in each st across. (202 sts)

Row 2: in B, dc 1 in each st across.

Row 3: in A, dc 2, *tr 1, dc 9, tr 2, dc 9, tr 1; rep from *, dc 2.

Row 4: in B, dc 2, *dc 1, tr 1, dc 3, tr 1, dc 3, tr 1, dc 2, tr 1, dc 3, tr 1, dc 3, tr 1, dc 1; rep from *, dc 2.

Row 5: in A, dc 2, *tr 1, dc 3, tr 1, dc 1, tr 1, dc 3, tr 2, dc 3, tr 1, dc 1, tr 1, dc 3, tr 1; rep from *, dc 2.

Row 6: in B, dc 2. *dc 5, tr 1, dc 10, tr 1, dc 5; rep from *, dc 2.

Row 7: in A, dc 1 in each st across.

Row 8: in B, dc 1 in each st across.

Row 9: in A, dc 12, *tr 2, dc 20, tr 2; rep from *, dc 12.

Row 10: in C, dc 11, tr 1, dc 2, tr 1, *dc 10, tr 1, dc 2, tr 1; rep from *, dc 11.

Row 11: in A, dc 10, tr 1, dc 4, tr 1, *dc 16, tr 1, dc 4, tr 1; rep from *, dc 10.

Row 12: in C, dc 9, tr 1, dc 6, tr 1, *dc 14, tr 1, dc 6, tr 1; rep from *, dc 9.

Row 13: in A, dc 8, tr 1, dc 8, tr 1, *dc 12, tr 1, dc 8, tr 1; rep from *, dc 8.

Row 14: in C, dc 7, tr 1, dc 10, tr 1, *dc 10, tr 1, dc 10, tr 1; rep from *, dc 7.

Row 15: in A, dc 6, tr 1, dc 12, tr 1, *dc 8, tr 1, dc 12, tr 1; rep from *, dc 6.

Row 16: in C, dc 5, tr 1, dc 14, tr 1, *dc 6, tr 1, dc 14, tr 1; rep from *, dc 5.

Row 17: in A, dc 4, tr 1, dc 16, tr 1, *dc 4, tr 1, dc 16, tr 1; rep from *, dc 4.

Row 18: in D, dc 3, tr 1, dc 18, tr 1, *dc 2, tr 1, dc 18, tr 1; rep from *, dc 3.

Row 19: in A, dc 2, tr 1, dc 20, *tr 2, dc 20; rep from * tr 1, dc 2.

Use A for all odd-numbered rows, D for Rows 20, 22 and 24, E for Row 26 and Row 28.

Rows 20–29: rep in reverse **Rows 18–9**.

Rows 30–39: rep **Rows 10–19**. Use A for all odd-numbered rows, E for Row 30, F for Rows 32, 34, 36 and 38.

Rows 40–49: rep in reverse **Rows 18–9**. Use A for all odd-numbered rows, G for Rows 40, 42, 44 and 46, H for Row 48.

Rows 50–51: rep **Row 2**. Use H for Row 50, A for Row 51.

Rows 52–54: rep in reverse **Rows 6–4**. Use H for Rows 52 and 54, A for Row 53.

Row 55: in A, htr 1 in each st across.

Fasten off (see Troubleshooting: Weaving in Ends).

FOR THE FRINGING

Tie the yarn ends of every 2 rows together to create fringing (see General Techniques: Edgings and Embellishments); dampen and trim to equal lengths.

Block (see Finishing Up: Blocking).

OVERLAY CROCHET

Many patterns use raised stitches to create interesting and decorative textures. Overlay crochet, however, is slightly different as the background stitches are usually worked in the back loops only (BLO) – or front loops only (FLO) when working in rows – leaving the loops on the right side free for stitches to be anchored to, in a similar method to mosaic crochet. Longer stitches such as double and triple trebles are used to reach several rows below, but unlike in mosaic work these stitches can be made diagonally, too. Overlay crochet is often used in mandala-making, where colour changes and stitch variations create beautiful, circular patterns in the round.

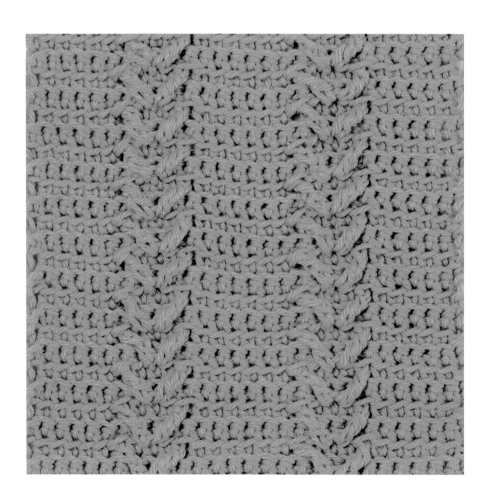

SPRIG OVERLAY CHART

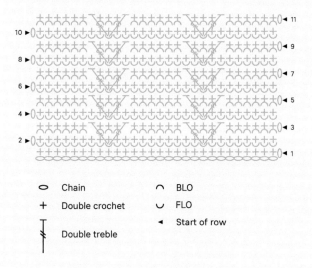

○	Chain	⌒	BLO
+	Double crochet	⌄	FLO
⟊	Double treble	◄	Start of row

> You may need to adjust the height of your stitch as you work to make it the same level as the surrounding stitches. This can be done easily when you draw the yarn through the stitch.

MAKING OVERLAY CROCHET

To make the overlay stitches really stand out, use shorter stitches as your background; the sample uses double crochet stitches behind the sprig relief. When crocheting the set-up rows, work all odd-numbered rows in the back loops only (see Basic Stitches: Working in Back Loops Only/Front Loops Only), and all the even-numbered ones in the front loops only. (When working in the round, the right side is always facing you, so all the double crochet stitches are BLO.)

To create the overlay stitch, wrap the yarn around the hook as many times as needed for the stitch – as this sample uses double trebles, you'll need to yarn over twice (A). Next, insert the hook into the unused front loop of the designated stitch (B), then complete the stitch as usual (C). Continue the pattern until the next overlay stitch is required.

CHARTED INSTRUCTIONS

In the sample, overlay stitches of double trebles are worked diagonally to create a sprig pattern. The chart (see above left) shows Rows 1–11.

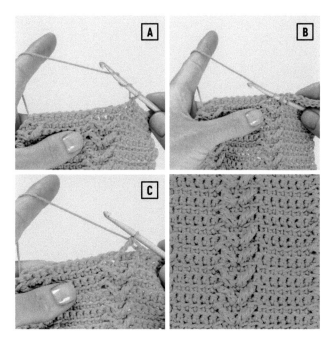

PATTERN

Ch 29.

Row 1: dc 1 in 2nd ch from hook, dc 1 in each st across, turn. (28 sts)

Row 2: ch 1, dc 1 FLO in each st across, turn.

Row 3: ch 1, *dc 6 BLO, dtr 1 in FLO of 9th (20th) st in Row 1, dc 3 BLO, dtr 1 in FLO of 9th (20th) from Row 1; rep from *, dc 6 BLO, turn.

Row 4: ch 1, dc 1 FLO in each st across, turn.

Rows 5–24: rep Rows 3–4 ten times, working dtrs in 9th (20th) st from 2 rows below.

MAHAYANA MANDALA

Mandala-making is often used as an aid to relaxation and meditation, and these mesmerising motifs are a popular project for many crocheters to play with overlay stitches and harmonious colours.

I USED

YARN

Anchor Creativa Fino (100% Cotton / 50g / 137yds/125m)

+ Yarn A: Grey (428); 1 ball
+ Yarn B: Pale Pink (409); 1 ball
+ Yarn C: Pink (114); 1 ball
+ Yarn D: Blue (384); 1 ball
+ Yarn E: Green (389); 1 ball

HOOKS AND ACCESSORIES

+ 3mm hook
+ Tapestry needle

FINISHED SIZE

26 x 26cm (10¼ x 10¼in) square approx

YOU COULD USE

Any similar 4-ply weight yarn and suitable hook

TENSION

Not essential to this project

Depending on your tension, you may need to adjust the number of chain stitches you make throughout the pattern to prevent your mandala from curling. This won't affect the appearance of the finished piece, as the chain stitches are worked over and encased by the stitches in the following round.

FURTHER STITCH VARIATIONS

Use a standing stitch at the beginning of each round (see Troubleshooting: Standing Stitch): for a treble, make a standing stitch and ch 1; for a double treble, a standing stitch and ch 2. For the neatest results, use the invisible fastening off method at the end of each round (see Troubleshooting: Invisible Fastening Off).

To make a popcorn stitch, see Stitch Variations: Popcorn Stitch. For a dtrPopcorn, make the stitch as a regular popcorn, but with 5 double trebles.

To make front post double treble 2 together (fpdtr2tog), work a fpdtr (see Basic Stitches: Front Post Treble) until the last yarn over, make a second fpdtr until the last yarn over, then yarn over and pull through all the remaining loops to complete the stitch.

MAHAYANA MANDALA STITCH CHART

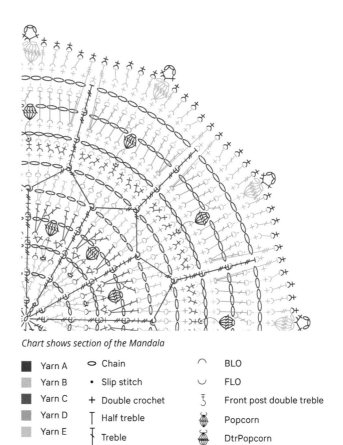

Chart shows section of the Mandala

■ Yarn A	⬭ Chain		⌒ BLO		
▦ Yarn B	• Slip stitch		⌣ FLO		
▦ Yarn C	+ Double crochet		⌠ Front post double treble		
▦ Yarn D	T Half treble		Popcorn		
▦ Yarn E	Treble		DtrPopcorn		
	Double treble		Triple treble		

PATTERN

Bracketed text following yarn indicates where to join yarn.

Rnd 1: in A, ch 4 (counts as 1ch and 1tr), tr 11 in 4th ch from hook. (12 tr)

Rnd 2: in B, 2tr BLO in each st around. (24 tr)

Rnd 3: in A (working around sts from Rnd 1), *fpdtr 1, ch 2; rep from * around. (12 fpdtr, 24 ch)

Rnd 4: in B (in any fpdtr from Rnd 3 and working in BLO), *tr 1, 3tr over the 2ch-sp and into one st from Rnd 2; rep from * around. (48 tr)

Rnd 5: in A (around fpdtr from Rnd 3), *fpdtr 1, ch 4; rep from * around. (12 fpdtr, 48 ch)

Rnd 6: in C (in any fpdtr from Rnd 5 and working in BLO), *dc 1, 2dc in one st, dc 1 in next st, dc 2 in next st over the 2ch-sp and into the sts from Rnd 4; rep from * around. (72 dc)

Rnd 7: in A (around fpdtr from Rnd 5), fptr 1, ch 2, popcorn in FLO of central tr of each 3tr group from Rnd 4, ch 2; rep from * around. (12 fptr, 12 popcorn, 48 ch)

Rnd 8: in C (in any fptr from Rnd 7 and working in BLO), *tr 1, 2tr over the 2ch-sp into first dc from Rnd 6, tr 1 over 2ch-sp and into first ch after popcorn, 2tr over the 2ch-sp into last dc from Rnd 6 before next fptr; rep from * around. (72 tr)

Rnd 9: in A (around fptr from Rnd 7), *fptr 1, ch 5; rep from * around. (12 fptr, 60 ch)

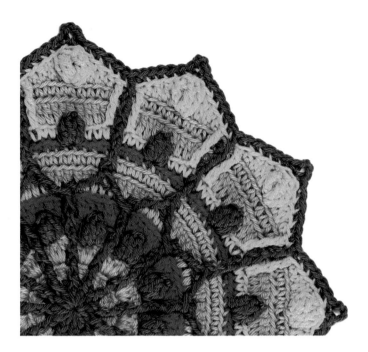

Rnd 10: in B (in any fptr from Rnd 9 and working in BLO), tr 1, 2tr over the 5ch-sp into 1st tr from Rnd 8, tr 3, 2tr in next tr from Rnd 8; rep from * around. (96 tr)

Rnd 11: in A (around any fptr from Rnd 9), ch 3, fpdtr 1 around next fptr (counts as fpdtr2tog), ch 6, *fpdtr2tog around each pair of fptrs from Rnd 9, ch 6; rep from * around. (12 fpdtr2tog, 72 ch)

Rnd 12: in D (in any fpdtr2tog from Rnd 11 and working in BLO), dc 1, dc 7 over the 6ch-sp into sts from Rnd 10; rep from * around. (96 dc)

Rnd 13: in C (in any dc above a fpdtr2tog and working in BLO), *dc 1, 2dc in next st, dc 5, 2dc in next st; rep from * around. (120 dc)

Rnd 14: in A (around any fpdtr2tog from Rnd 11), *fpdtr 1, ch 11; rep from * around. (12 fpdtr, 132 ch)

Rnd 15: in E (in fpdtr from Rnd 14 and working in BLO), *dc 1, dc 9 over the 11ch-sp into sts from Rnd 13; rep from * around. (120 dc)

Rnd 16: in A (around any fpdtr from Rnd 14), *fptr 1, ch 4, popcorn in FLO of 5th dc after fpdtr from Rnd 13, ch 4; rep from * around. (12 fptr, 12 popcorn, 96 ch)

Rnd 17: in D (in fpdtr from Rnd 16 and working in BLO), *tr 1, 2tr in next dc from Rnd 9, tr 3, tr 1 in 1st ch after popcorn, tr 3, 2tr in next dc from Rnd 9, all worked over 4ch-sp; rep from * around. (144 tr)

Rnd 18: in A (around any fpdtr from Rnd 16), *fptr 1, ch 10; rep from * around. (12 fptr, 120 ch)

Rnd 19: in B (in fpdtr from Rnd 18 and working in BLO), dc 1 in each st around, working over 10ch-sp and into sts from Rnd 17. (144 dc)

Rnd 20: in E (in the FLO of any dc of Rnd 15, directly after fptr), *ttr 1, (now working in sts from Rnd 19, in BLO) htr 1, tr 2, dtr 1, dtrPopcorn, ch 1, dtr 1, tr 2, htr 1, sl st, ttr 1 into FLO of dc of Rnd 15, directly before fptr; rep from * around. (12 popcorn, 24 ttr, 24 dtr, 48 tr, 24 htr, 12 ch)

Rnd 21: in A (in the BLO of the ch after a dtrPopcorn from Rnd 20), *(dc 1, ch 3, dc 1) in same st, dc 5 BLO, fptr 1 (around fptr from Rnd 18), dc 5 BLO; rep from * around. (144 dc, 36 ch, 12 fptr)

Fasten off and weave in ends (see Troubleshooting: Weaving in Ends).

Block (see Finishing Up: Blocking).

Loosely translated from the Sanskrit for circle, mandalas traditionally symbolise the universe in a microcosm.

CROCHET EMBROIDERY

Crochet is the perfect background for embroidery, meaning you can add decoration and detail to areas of the surface of your project. You can embellish crochet fabrics with ease, and the short, dense stitches of double crochet and Tunisian crochet work particularly well with this technique. Choose whichever thread or yarn you like for sewing, and add beads, sequins or other interesting embellishments, just as you would with any other embroidered project.

CROSS STITCH

It's simple to make a cross stitch on double crochet as the crochet stitches themselves are almost square in shape. Working from the back, bring your needle up into one corner of the square and down diagonally in the opposite corner to completes the first 'leg' of the cross. Bring your needle back up into the next corner in line with your previous stitch, then diagonally across and through to the wrong side (A). For a row of cross stitches, methodically work the first row of diagonal legs, then work back across the row to complete the stitches.

CHAIN STITCH

Bring your needle through to the front of your work and back down just next to the first hole, leaving a small loop. Now bring the needle back to the front, a short distance along from the first two holes (the length you want your stitch to be), and catch the loop from the first stitch. This anchors the stitch and forms the first chain (B). To make the next chain stitch, take your needle back down, just next to this new hole to create a new loop, and repeat.

BACKSTITCH

Make a single stitch by bringing your needle from the back to the front of your work and through to the back again – you can make this stitch as long or short as needed. Next, bring up your needle a stitch length away, as if you were making a running stitch (C). Complete the stitch by working back into the last hole created by the first stitch (D), then bring your needle up again one length along. This forms an almost solid line of stitches on the right side, and a line of oversewn stitches on the wrong side.

FRENCH KNOT

Bring your needle up through the fabric a short way and wrap the thread around the shaft once or more, depending on how large you want the knot. Insert the needle back into the fabric very close to the hole, then gently pull the needle and working thread back down through the wrapped loops to leave a knot on the surface (E).

BLANKET STITCH

This stitch is often worked around the edges of a project. First, secure your thread so you have a vertical loop over the edge and you can work from left to right. Make a loose diagonal stitch across the back and bring the needle out at the front, a short distance from the edge (F). Take the needle down vertically and through the loose loop of the diagonal back stitch (G). Pull gently, so the loop lies flat along the bottom edge to complete the stitch. To continue, make another diagonal stitch across the back.

SATIN STITCH

Also known as damask stitch, this is a dense embroidery stitch that is used to completely cover or colour in a section of a design. To create the stitch, work straight stitches next to each other, keeping the threads flat and the edges neat, filling in the shape (H).

FOLK ART EMBROIDERY

Use embroidery to transform a plain fabric of double crochet and create a folk-inspired piece of art. Use the chart as a guide, bearing in mind you may want to work some embroidery stitches over more than one crochet stitch.

I USED

YARN

Rico Creative Cotton Aran (100% Cotton / 50g / 93yds/85m)

+ Main Yarn: Dark Blue (38); 1 ball
Ricorumi DK (100% Cotton / 25g / 63yds/58m)

+ Yarn A: White (01); small amount
+ Yarn B: Yellow (06); small amount
+ Yarn C: Raspberry (13); small amount
+ Yarn D: Red (28); small amount
+ Yarn E: Sky Blue (31); small amount
+ Yarn F: Green (49); small amount

HOOKS AND ACCESSORIES

+ 4mm hook
+ Tapestry needle

FINISHED SIZE

21 x 25cm (8¼ x 10in) approx

YOU COULD USE

Any weight yarn or embroidery threads and suitable hook or needle

TENSION

Not essential to this project

FOLK ART EMBROIDERY CHART

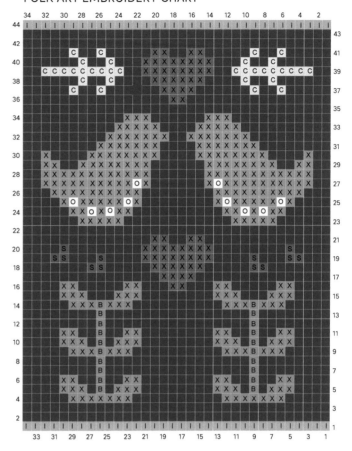

X = Cross stitch
C = Chain stitch
S = Satin stitch
I = Blanket stitch
O = French knots
B = Back stitch

Main Yarn
Yarn A
Yarn B
Yarn C
Yarn D
Yarn E
Yarn F

PATTERN

In Main Yarn, ch 34.

Row 1: ch 1, dc 1 in 2nd ch from hook, dc 1 in each st across, turn. (34 sts)

Rows 2-44: ch 1, dc 1 in 2nd st from hook, dc 1 in each st across, turn.

Fasten off and weave in ends (see Troubleshooting: Weaving in Ends).

Block (see Finishing Up: Blocking).

Follow the chart to add the embroidery; each square represents one double crochet stitch.

Fill the stems by stitching 3 rows of backstitch, making your stitches overlap slightly to create a solid colour.

SURFACE CROCHET

This technique is a great way to add extra definition and pattern to a piece of existing crochet. You can use it to emphasise the edges of a design, create a sharp border for a blanket, or go freestyle and make organic shapes and swirls. Surface crochet is usually made using a slip stitch, giving a similar effect to an embroidered chain stitch, but you can experiment with others, of course. The surface stitches themselves work best when applied to a crocheted piece where the stitches are packed closely together, and you'll find it easiest to work into the natural gaps between the stitches, utilising the existing holes in the piece.

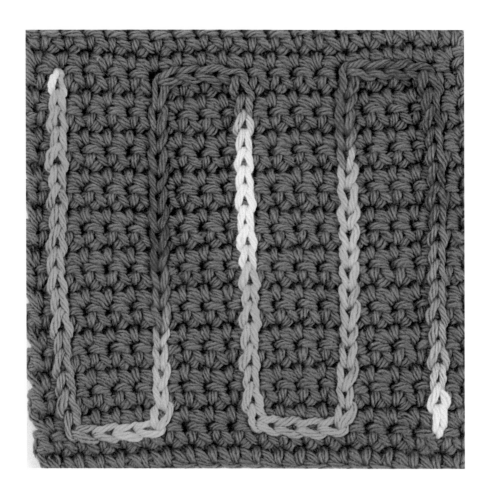

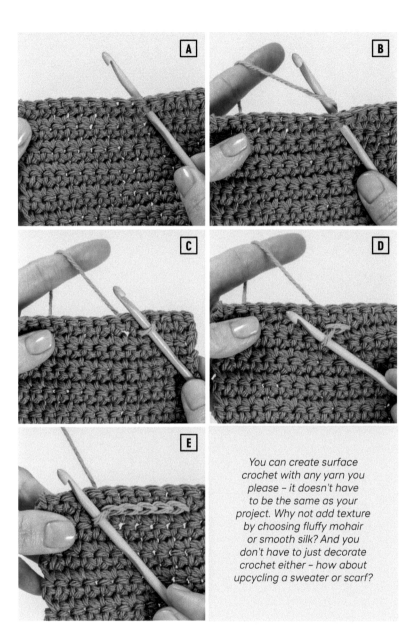

You can create surface crochet with any yarn you please – it doesn't have to be the same as your project. Why not add texture by choosing fluffy mohair or smooth silk? And you don't have to just decorate crochet either – how about upcycling a sweater or scarf?

MAKING SURFACE CROCHET

It's usually best to work across one stitch at a time so that these slip stitches are the same length as those in your crochet piece, but again it's up to you.

1. To make surface crochet, begin with the right side of the crochet piece facing you. Insert your hook where you are going to begin, remembering that you'll be working from **right** to **left** (A).

2. With the working yarn behind the crochet, pull up a loop, leaving a good length tail for securing the end later (B and C).

3. Insert your hook into where the next stitch should go. Yarn over (behind your work), and draw the yarn through the crochet and through the loop on your hook to complete the stitch (D).

4. Repeat Step 3, keeping your slip stitches as neat and even as you can. You don't have to work in a straight line – the beauty of this technique is that you can turn to work in any direction (E).

AMMONITE COASTERS

Inspired by a collection of beautiful fossils from Lyme Regis, these coasters really show off a colour-changing yarn in a detailing of surface crochet that accentuates the graceful curves.

I USED

YARN

Lily Sugar 'n Cream Solids (100% Cotton / 71g / 119yds/109m)

+ Yarn A: Overcast (01042); 1 ball
Lily Sugar 'n Cream Ombre (100% Cotton / 55g / 94yds/86m)

+ Yarn B: Psychedelic Ombre (02660); 1 ball

NEEDLES AND ACCESSORIES

+ 5mm hook
+ Stitch marker
+ Tapestry needle

FINISHED SIZE

10 x 9cm (4 x 3½in)

YOU COULD USE

Any similar Aran or worsted weight yarn and suitable hook

TENSION

Not essential to this project

These Coasters are made in continuous rounds. Use a stitch marker to mark the first stitch of the round and you won't get lost.

PATTERN

Rnd 1: in A, ch 2 (doesn't count as a st), htr 10 in 2nd ch from hook. (10 sts)

Rnd 2: 2htr in each st around. (20 sts)

Rnd 3: (htr 1, 2htr in next st), rep around. (30 sts)

Rnd 4: (htr 2, 2htr in next st) 8 times, (tr 1, 2tr in next st) 3 times. (41 sts)

Rnd 5 (short round): tr 2 (leave 39 sts unworked).

Fasten off.

SURFACE CROCHET

Using B, insert the hook into the centre of the Coaster and draw up a loop. Working in the spaces between the rounds, make one sl st in each stitch around, until you reach the end of the spiral, then tr 1 in the same stitch as the last treble from Rnd 5.

Fasten off and weave in ends (see Troubleshooting: Weaving in Ends).

AMMONITE COASTER STITCH CHART

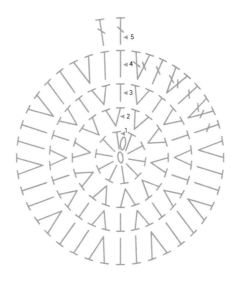

⌒	Chain
⊤	Half Treble
⊤̸	Treble
◄	Start of round

As a variation, reverse the colours

FILET CROCHET

Here we have a straightforward method of creating patterns and pictures based on a grid of squares, some are solid and filled with stitches, while others are left as open spaces. The designs for filet work can be amazingly intricate – using fine-weight yarns can replicate traditional lace patterns, while weightier yarns appear more graphic and modern by producing bold, striking designs. Typically, a set number of trebles and chains are used to create the solid or open blocks, and it is the arrangement of these on the grid that creates the overall design.

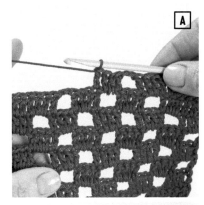

You may find it easier to think of a block as comprising just three stitches: a solid block is 3 trebles (A); an open block is 1 treble and 2 chains (B). Expect to see an extra stitch to complete the side for an open block at the end of a row.

WORKING FILET CROCHET

Filet crochet patterns are drawn as charts – usually in rows – that show filled or open blocks, and they are read from the bottom to the top. All odd-numbered rows are worked from right to left and the even-numbered rows from left to right.

The pattern gives instructions for how many stitches make up one block; in the sample, one block is 2 trebles, with 2 stitches between. The block can be filled with 2 trebles (A), or left open with 2 chains, then, to keep the linear look, the next 2 stitches are skipped before starting the next solid block (B). The trebles on each side of each block are 'shared', so the stitch count for each row is a multiple of 3, plus 1 extra stitch.

FILET CROCHET STITCH CHART

This stitch chart shows the arrangement of trebles and chains from a section of the chart

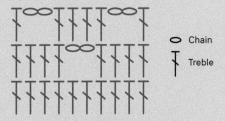

○ Chain

⊤ Treble

FILET CROCHET SAMPLE GRID

This grid shows the arrangement of blocks for the sample, with the white blocks representing those with 2 chains

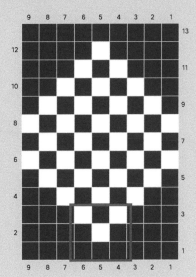

TEATIME PLACEMAT

Filet crochet is used here to create a striking yet simple-to-make table accessory. Worked in rows of trebles in a gorgeous DK cotton, this mat is durable and fun!

I USED

YARN

Patons 100% Cotton DK (100% Cotton / 100g / 230yds/210m): Royal (2751); 2 balls

HOOKS AND ACCESSORIES

+ 3mm hook

FINISHED SIZE

48 x 33cm (18¾ x 13in) approx

YOU COULD USE

Any DK cotton yarn and suitable hook to match gauge

TENSION

10 x 10cm (4 x 4in) square: 19 sts and 9.5 rows (using 3mm hook measured over pattern)

PATTERN

The blocks for this pattern are 2 trebles with one stitch between. Use the grid (below) to follow the pattern, working from right to left for the odd-numbered rows and left to right for the even-numbered ones.

Ch 88.

Rows 1–29: ch 3 (counts as 1 tr throughout), follow chart working tr 3 for each solid block and (tr 1, sk one st, ch 1, tr 1) for each white block, turn. (89 sts)

When you have finished the last row, do not fasten off, but work around the edge in an anti-clockwise direction to add an edging.

Row 30: ch 1, dc 1 evenly along each side, with 2ch in each corner.

Fasten off and weave in ends (see Troubleshooting: Weaving in Ends).

Block (see Finishing Up: Blocking).

TEATIME PLACEMAT GRID

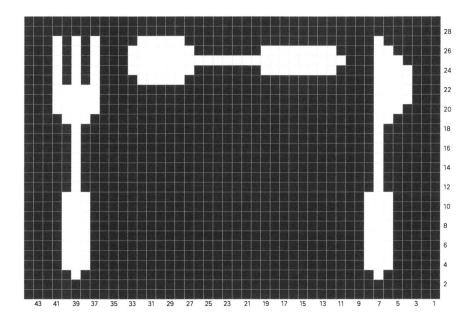

PLANNED COLOUR-POOLING

This technique is a fun way of working with variegated yarn and manipulates colour-changing yarn to create an incredible Argyle-effect pattern, where the colours appear to cross over each other in diagonal stripes. Achieving this is relatively easy using linen stitch, but requires a little patience and some tinkering with tension as you work. To try planned colour-pooling, you need to choose either a yarn manufactured for this purpose, or one that has equal lengths of colour change.

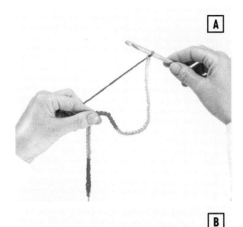

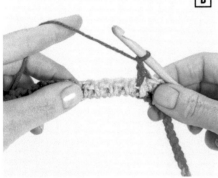

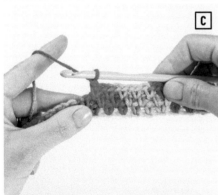

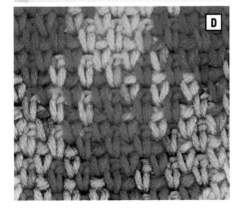

HOW TO POOL COLOURS

1. Make a foundation chain long enough to work through all the colours, finishing with 1 loop of the first colour on the hook (A).

2. Row 1: dc 1 in 4th chain from hook. Continue the first row: *1 ch, sk 1 ch, dc 1 in the next stitch; rep from * across, until you have completed one set of colour changes (you won't crochet across the entire chain, but that's fine as you can unpick the extra stitches when you have finished). For the colour-pooling to work, you need to unpick 1 dc and 1 ch, then turn. In this sample, the colour change every 3 stitches, so there are only 2 dc at the end of the row in the final colour.

3. Row 2: ch 2, dc 1 in the 1ch-sp (this stitch will be the last one in the final colour and the next stitch will be the first colour again) (B). Continue in linen stitch: *ch 1, dc 1 in 1ch-sp; rep from * across row, turn (C).

4. Row 3: rep **Row 2**. This is the row where you should notice the colours from Row 1 appear to move across by 1 stitch on every row. If not, you'll need to pull back your work and adjust the tension of your stitches so that you have more or less of a colour on your hook. If your pattern is working, continue the row (D).

COMMON ISSUES

The difficulty with colour-pooling is in the length of the stitches – the ch 2 at the beginning of each row uses less yarn than a double crochet, so you may end up with one edge that works perfectly, and one that doesn't. If this happens, there are a few easy things to try. One option is to adjust your tension – perhaps try working with a larger hook or relaxing your stitches. Another method is to replace a couple of the double crochet stitches with a half treble. This helps use up a bit more of the yarn without adjusting the tension, and because the stitches look similar, it isn't obvious.

You may notice a small gap in your project when working into the chain space from the previous row if the surrounding stitches were half trebles. To make these holes less visible, make your next stitch into the top of the stitch below.

A REALLY, REALLY, REALLY LONG SCARF

With its rainbow hues running in diagonal lines across the project, this scarf puts colour-pooling through its paces.

I USED

YARN

Red Heart Super Saver Pooling
(100% Acrylic / 141g / 235yds/215m):
Papaya (8536); 3 balls

HOOKS AND ACCESSORIES

+ 4.5mm hook
+ Tapestry needle

FINISHED SIZE

18 x 272cm (7in x 3yd) approx

YOU COULD USE

Any colour-pooling yarn and suitable
hook

TENSION

Adjust if necessary (see Planned
Colour-Pooling: How to Pool Colours)

PATTERN

If you want to add fringing to your project,
get these ready first so you don't run out of
yarn. Cut around 120 strands, each measuring
approx 25–30cm (10–12in).

Work through the Planned Colour-pooling
technique for getting started with your scarf.

Make ch to 2 sts before end of last colour
change.

Row 1: dc 1 in 4th ch from hook, ch 1, *sk 1 ch,
dc 1 in next st; rep from * across, turn.

Row 2: ch 2, dc 1 in 1ch-sp, *ch 1, dc 1 in next
1ch-sp; rep from * to end.

Row 3 onwards: rep **Row 2**, until you can finish
the last row with your remaining yarn.

Fasten off and weave in ends (see
Troubleshooting: Weaving in Ends).

FOR THE FRINGING

Divide the strands for fringing into threes,
and fold each set in half. Use your hook to
loop them through the chain spaces across
the short edges of the scarf (see Edgings and
Embellishments: Fringing). Trim.

SUPER-SIZE CROCHET

New manufacturing capabilities have meant that giant yarn is now available in both luxurious merino wool, as well as more affordable and robust acrylic versions. Due to the way it's produced, these mega yarns are described as roving. This means they are not plied or twisted and therefore need to be worked with care, otherwise the strands can weaken and even break. These oversized yarns lend themselves well to projects with a wow factor. You could upsize a pattern to create a rug or make a stunning wall hanging based on a traditional granny square – the best thing is that they can be created in no time.

CROCHETING WITH YOUR FINGERS

Using giant yarn to crochet with is good fun, but trying to wield a ginormous hook can be a little daunting, not to mention awkward, so why not use your fingers instead? It takes a bit of practice to even out the tension, but once you get the feel for it, you'll find it really is quite easy.

1. To start, simply make a slip knot and foundation chain as usual (A).

2. Pull the yarn gently through each chain you make (B).

3. To make a double crochet, insert your thumb and first finger into the stitch (C).

4. Next, ease the yarn through to make 2 loops held by your fingers (D), then yarn over and pull the yarn through again to complete the stitch (E).

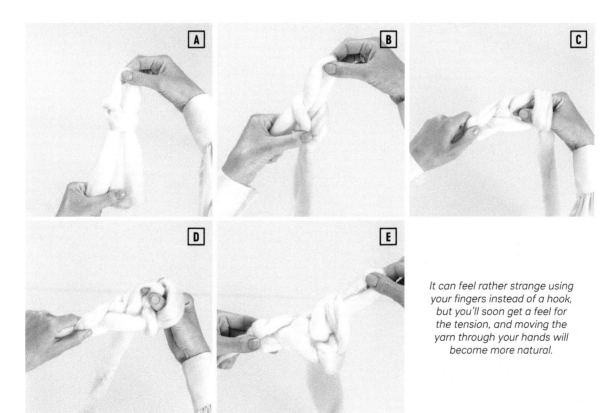

It can feel rather strange using your fingers instead of a hook, but you'll soon get a feel for the tension, and moving the yarn through your hands will become more natural.

FESTIVE WREATH

This project is the simplest in the book and is going to take very little time to complete – don't worry if you haven't got a great big hook, you can use your fingers instead.

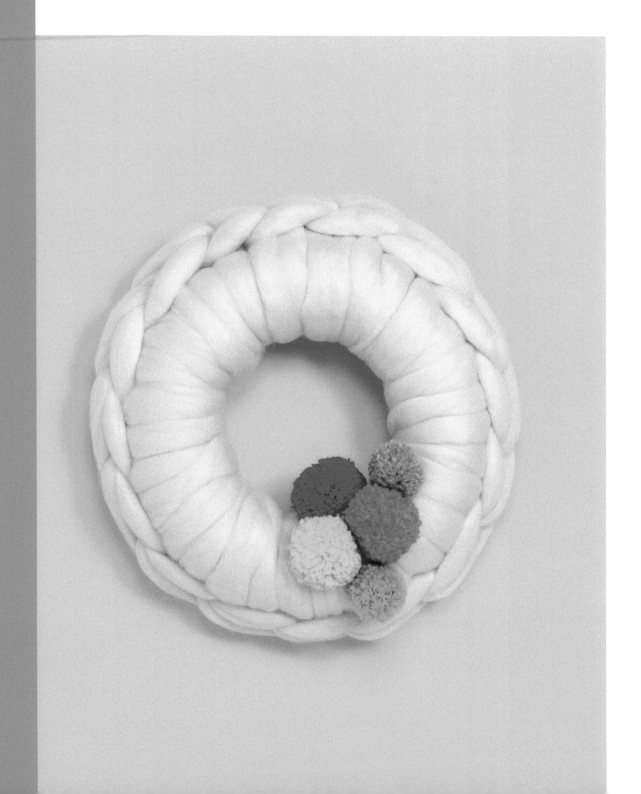

I USED

YARN

Woolly Mahoosive 19.5 Micron Superfine Giant Merino (100% Merino / 1kg / 40m/44yds): Cream; 1 ball (you only need 200g to make this wreath)

HOOKS AND ACCESSORIES

+ 40mm hook (or fingers)
+ 25cm (10in) polystyrene ring
+ 45mm (1¾in) pompoms made from assorted leftover yarn for decorations

FINISHED SIZE

30 x 30cm (12 x 12in)

YOU COULD USE

Any similar super-size yarn and suitable hook, or your fingers

TENSION

Not essential to this project

PATTERN

Begin with a slip knot on your hook (or fingers). Holding the polystyrene wreath in your left hand, you'll now work just a single row of wrap double crochet stitches around the wreath.

Row 1: *insert the hook into the middle of the ring, yarn over and draw the yarn through to the front, yarn over and draw the yarn through, creating the 'V' of the stitch around the outside of the wreath; rep from * to cover the wreath without any gaps.

Fasten off and weave in ends (see Troubleshooting: Weaving in Ends).

MULTI-STRAND OMBRÉ CROCHET

There are, of course, commercially produced yarns that produce gradual colour changes for you, but it's good fun to experiment and create your own ombré effect using yarn from your stash. To do this, you need to work with two strands at a time and use a slightly larger hook to compensate. You can achieve this fantastic effect with any stitch combination you like and can work in rows or rounds, making it an extremely versatile technique.

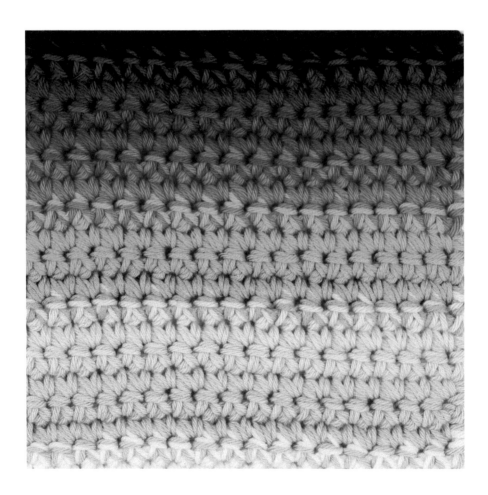

WORKING WITH MULTIPLE STRANDS

In this sample, double crochet stitches are used with various colours of the same yarn, with 1 strand being substituted on every row.

1. First, work one row using both strands of your Yarn A (A).

2. On the next row, drop 1 strand of A and pick up 1 strand of B (B).

3. Crochet the next row using these different colours together, then at the end drop A and pick up a second strand of B to work across the third row (C).

4. For the next row drop 1 strand of B and pick up 1 strand of C (D).

Continue to change colours in this way for a continuous colour change.

It's entirely up to you when you make the colour changes and how many strands to work with – and, of course, what colours you choose to blend. Choose yarns of a similar tone to create a gradual ombré effect, or why not try clashing colour combinations for some surprising effects?

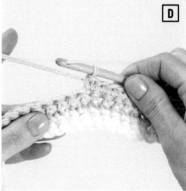

CROCHET RIBBING AND CABLES

Most people associate ribs and cables with knitting, but you can create a similar effect in crochet – great news for adding stretchy edgings to wearables and vertical textured patterns to just abut anything you like. You'll be amazed at how easy it is to make ribbing, and expect to see a stitch chart to help with cable patterns.

RIBBING SAMPLE

CABLE SAMPLE

RIBBING

Ribbing is an important element of garment construction and provides an edge that is form-fitting, being elastic and returning to its shape after being stretched. You probably already know the techniques to work a rib, the most effective being to work in rows in the back loops only (see Basic Stitches: Working in Back Loops Only/Front Loops Only). Shorter stitches work best and create a neat, stretchy fabric.

DIFFERENT RIB STYLES

The ribbing sample shown opposite demonstrates three different ribs, but for each one the stitches have been worked in rows in the back loops only. You can see that using slip stitches (on the left) creates a very tight and closely formed rib, closer to a knitted rib, while using slightly taller stitches makes a more relaxed and looser style.

MAKING RIBBING

1. Make a foundation chain of a length to matches the **height** of ribbing that you want (A).

2. Ch 1, turn, then work across in your chosen stitch, turn (B).

3. Now working in BLO, continue to crochet until the rib is the desired **length** to fit around your project (C).

Remember that ribbing will stretch, so make it reasonably well-fitting as it may get looser over time.

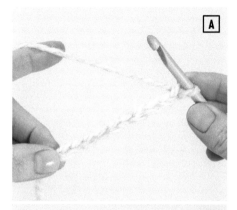

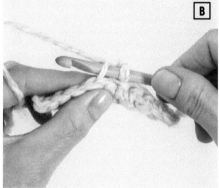

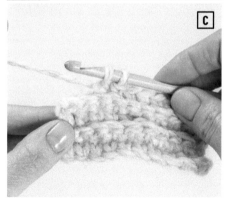

CABLES

Cables are used for a decorative effect, producing a raised pattern in which columns of stitches appear to twist around each other. The patterns may look complex, but don't be put off, as they are crocheted by simply overlaying longer stitches with front post stitches (see Basic Stitches: Front Post Treble).

MAKING A CABLE

Ch 16.

Rows 1 and 2: ch 1 (does not count as a stitch), dc 1 in each st across, turn. (A)

Row 3: ch 1, dc 6, fptr 4 (around sts 2 rows directly below), dc 6, turn. (B and C)

Row 4: ch 1, dc 1 in each st across, turn.

Row 5: ch 1, dc 6, sk 2 sts, fpdtr 2 (around fptrs two rows below), then working back across the front of 2 skipped sts: fpdtr 2 (around fptrs 2 rows below), dc 6, turn. (D, E and F)

CABLE SAMPLE CHART

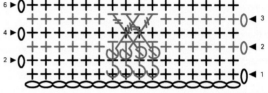

○ Chain
+ Double crochet
⊤ Treble
⌇ Front post treble
⌇ Front post double treble
◄ Start of row

Row 6: rep **Row 2**.

Row 7: rep **Row 3**.

Row 8: rep **Row 2**.

Row 9: rep **Row 5**.

Rows 10–17: rep **Rows 6–9** twice.

Row 18: rep **Row 6**.

Alternatively, continue to rep **Rows 6–9** until cable is desired length, then finish with a Row 6.

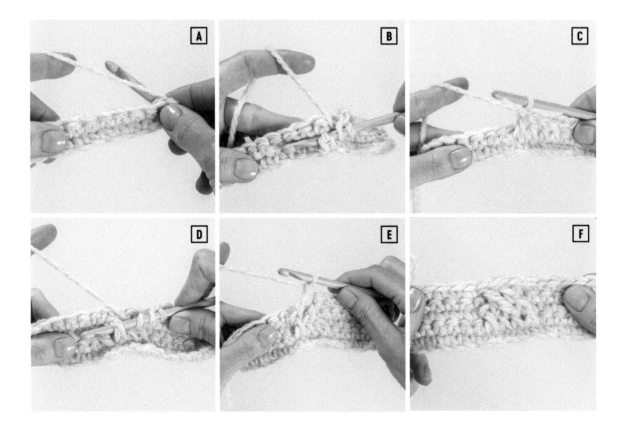

THE COSY CABLE HAT

Cabling creates a super-squishy fabric and so lends itself well to crochet items intended to keep you warm. Here, a hat is the perfect project, and it also incorporates a ribbed band for comfort and fit.

I USED

YARN

Jarol Shetland Mist Chunky
(80% Acrylic, 20% Wool / 100g /
164yds/150m): Soft Grey (06);
2 balls

HOOKS AND ACCESSORIES

+ 6 mm hook
+ Tapestry needle
+ Fur pompom

FINISHED SIZE

24 x 27cm (9½ x 10½in) approx

YOU COULD USE

Stylecraft Life Chunky or Hayfield
Chunky with Wool

TENSION

10 x 10cm (4 x 4in) square: 11 sts and
13 rows (using 6mm hook measured
over pattern)

PATTERN

The hat is made in one piece as a rectangle,
then the sides are seamed and the top
gathered to create the shape. It can be altered
to fit any head, just ensure that the number of
ribbing rows completed is a multiple of 6.

RIBBED BAND

Ch 8.

Row 1: ch 1 (does not count as a stitch), dc 1
BLO in 2nd ch from hook, dc 1 BLO in each st
across, turn. (8 sts)

Rows 2-60: ch 1 (does not count as a stitch),
dc 1 BLO in each st across, turn.

Do not fasten off, turn 90 degrees to work the
crown across the long edge of the band.

CROWN

Rows 61 and 62: ch 1, dc 1 in each st across,
turn. (60 sts)

Row 63: ch 1, dc 1, fptr 4 (around sts 2 rows
directly below), *dc 2, fptr 4 (around sts 2 rows
directly below); rep from * across until one st
remaining, dc 1, turn.

Row 64: ch 1, dc 1 in each st across, turn.

Row 65: ch 1, dc 1, sk 2 sts, fpdtr 2 (around
fptrs 2 rows below), then working across the
front of 2 skipped sts: fpdtr 2 (around fptrs
2 rows below), *dc 2, sk 2 sts, fpdtr 2 (around
fptrs 2 rows below), then working across the
front of 2 skipped sts, fpdtr 2 (around fptrs 2
rows below) across, until one st remaining,
dc 1, turn.

Row 66: rep **Row 64**.

Rows 67–90: rep **Rows 63, 64, 65, 64** six
times, ending on a Row 64.

Fasten off, leaving a length of 50cm for sewing
the seam. With RS facing, use whip stitch (see
Finishing Up: Joining Motifs and Edges) to
seam the side edges together.

Cut another length of yarn and sew a running
stitch around the top edge between the
stitches; pull gently to close the hole. Knot
securely and sew the pompom to the top.

Fasten off and weave in all ends (see
Troubleshooting: Weaving in Ends).

THE MARCHANT COWL

Inspired by Nancy Marchant and her extensive expertise in knitting brioche, this easy crocheted version produces a thick and cosy rib.

CROCHET BRIOCHE TECHNIQUE

Brioche is another technique closely related to ribbing. In knitted brioche, a reversible rib is created with layers of tucked stitches, which produces a super-thick and squishy fabric. The brioche effect can be achieved in crochet by working ribbing in the backs loop only (see Modern Techniques: Crochet Ribbing and Cables), or by making post stitches continuously, as in this must-make Cowl.

I USED

YARN

Drops Polaris (100% Wool / 100g / 39yds/36m): Off White (01); 3 balls

HOOKS AND ACCESSORIES

+ 15mm hook

FINISHED SIZE

35 x 17cm (13¾ x 6¾in) approx

YOU COULD USE

Any similar super chunky yarn and suitable hook to match gauge

TENSION

10 x 10cm (4 x 4in) square: 6 sts and 5 rows (using 15mm hook measured over pattern)

PATTERN

Ch 37, join with a sl st to first ch.

Rnd 1: ch 3, tr 1 in each st around, join with a sl st to top of 3ch.

Rnds 2–9: ch 2, fptr 1 in each st around, join with a sl st to top of 2ch.

Fasten off and weave in ends (see Troubleshooting: Weaving in Ends).

AMIGURUMI

Amigurumi crochet is a fun technique from Japan for making small, cute creations. Traditionally worked in the round, in a continuous spiral of stitches, this method produces a neat, seamless finish. Shaping is achieved by increasing and decreasing throughout the pattern, with limbs and other parts being made separately, then stuffed and sewn on at the end. The appeal of amigurumi makes, apart from their amusing quirkiness, is that they are quick to create and use just a handful of simple stitches – mostly double crochet.

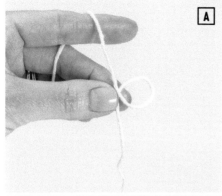

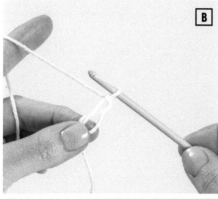

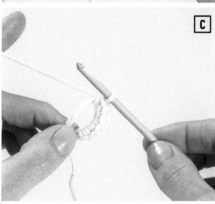

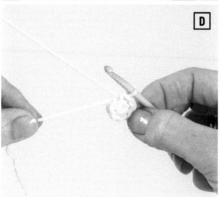

MAKING A MAGIC RING AND ROUND 1

The method of starting in the round for amigurumi is often the magic ring – so-called because the end can be pulled and tightened to give a tight centre with no hole at all. You might also see this called a magic circle or magic loop.

1. To begin the magic ring, make a loop with the yarn (A).

2. Insert the hook through the loop and pull the yarn through, then yarn over and pull it through once more (B).

3. Make dc 6 into the ring, working over the yarn tail at the same time to enclose it (C).

4. When you have completed the round, pull the yarn tail gently to close the hole (D).

ROUND 1 WITH CH 2

If you prefer, you can begin amigurumi in this way: ch 2, dc 6 into the 2nd ch from hook (E); pull the yarn tail to close the hole.

CONTINUING THE SAMPLE PATTERN

It's very easy to continue crocheting in amigurumi – there's no need to join rounds with a slip stitch, or make a starting chain, just carry on working around. It's a good idea to put a stitch marker in the first stitch, so you don't lose your place. Continue with the pattern, moving the stitch marker up at the start of every round:

Rnd 2: 2dc in each st around. (12 dc)

Rnd 3: (dc 1, 2dc in next st) around. (18 dc)

Rnd 4: (dc 2, 2dc in next st) around. (24 dc)

Rnd 5: (dc 3, 2dc in next st) around. (30 dc)

Rnd 6: (dc 4, 2dc in next st) around. (36 dc)

Rnd 7: (dc 5, 2dc in next st) around. (42 dc)

Rnds 8–13: dc 1 in each st around.

INVISIBLE DECREASE

This method of decreasing stitches is particularly useful in amigurumi as it creates a near-invisible stitch. To make stitches FLO or BLO see Basic Stitches: Working in Back Loops Only/Front Loops Only.

To dc2tog, insert your hook under the FLO of the first st, then the FLO of the second st (F), yarn over and draw through, yarn over and pull through to complete the stitch (G).

Rnd 14: (dc 5, dc2tog) around. (36 dc)

Rnd 15: (dc 4, dc2tog) around. (30 dc)

Rnd 16: (dc 3, dc2tog) around. (24 dc)

Rnd 17: (dc 2, dc2tog) around. (18 dc)

Stuff firmly with toy filling.

Rnd 18: (dc 1, dc2tog) around. (12 dc)

Rnd 19: (dc2tog) around. (6 dc)

Cut yarn, thread yarn tail onto a tapestry needle, pass through BLO of last round, draw up to close, then fasten off.

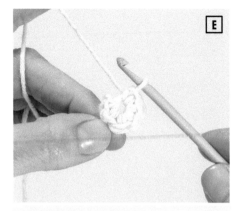

E

When making amigurumi in the round, the right side (with the 'V's) is always facing you. You may find that your project starts to curl inwards as you crochet, so make sure you turn it out the right way before stuffing.

F

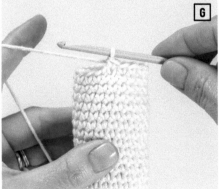

G

NO DRAMA LLAMA

Using basic amigurumi techniques, this llama won't give you any dramas. Crochet the pieces, assemble them together, then dress with extra surface details for a characterful creature.

I USED

YARN

Stylecraft Classique Cotton DK
(100% Cotton / 50g / 101yds/92m)

+ Yarn A: Ivory (3665); 2 balls
+ Yarn B: Fondant (3094); small
  amounts
+ Yarn C: Toffee (3656); small
  amounts
+ Yarn D: Wheat (3967); small
  amounts
+ Yarn E: Azure (3671); small
  amounts
+ Yarn F: Poppy (3672); small
  amounts
+ Yarn G: Fuchsia (3692); small
  amounts

HOOKS AND ACCESSORIES

+ 3.5mm hook
+ Tapestry needle
+ Toy filling
+ Sewing needle
+ Brown embroidery thread for eyes
  and nose

FINISHED SIZE

27 x 16cm (10½ x 6¼in) approx

YOU COULD USE

Any similar DK cotton yarn and
suitable hook

TENSION

Not essential to this project

*Leave long tails after fastening off for
sewing pieces together at the end.*

PATTERN

HEAD, NECK AND BODY

Stuff with toy filling as the parts take shape.

Rnd 1: in A, dc 5 in magic ring; or ch 2, dc 5 in 2nd ch
from hook. (5 sts)

Rnd 2: (2dc in each st) around. (10 sts)

Rnd 3: (dc 1, 2dc in next st) around. (15 sts)

Rnd 4: (dc 2, 2dc in next st) around. (20 sts)

Rnds 5–20: dc 1 in each st around.

Do not fasten off, but continue for Body.

Rnd 21: ch 17, dc 1 in each ch, 1 dc in each st of neck,
working back along opposite side of chain, dc 1 in each
ch (A). (54 sts)

Rnds 22–39: dc 1 in each st around.

Rnds 40–42: (dc 1, dc2tog) around. (16 sts)

Rnd 43: (dc2tog) around. (8 sts)

Cut yarn, thread yarn tail onto a tapestry needle, pass
through BLO of last round, draw up to close, then
fasten off.

TAIL

Rnd 1: in A, dc 4 in magic ring; or ch 2, dc 4 in 2nd ch
from hook. (4 sts)

Rnd 2: dc 1 in each st around.

Rnd 3: (dc 1, 2dc in next st) around. (6 sts)

Rnd 4: dc 1 in each st around.

Rnd 5: (dc 2, 2dc in next st) around. (8 sts)

Rnd 6: dc 1 in each st around.

Rnd 7: (dc2tog) around. (4 sts)

Cut yarn, thread yarn tail onto a tapestry needle, pass
through BLO of last round, draw up to close, then fasten
off. Sew to Body.

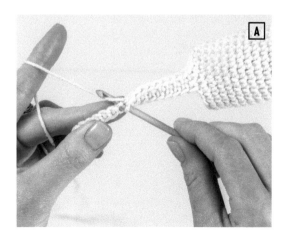

MUZZLE

Rnd 1: in D, dc 5 in magic ring; or ch 2, dc 5 in 2nd ch from hook. (5 sts)

Rnd 2: (2dc in each st) around. (10 sts)

Rnds 3–6: dc 1 in each st around.

Fasten off. Using brown embroidery thread in a sewing needle, embroider nose.

Stuff Muzzle and sew to Head (B).

Embroider eyes on Head.

EARS (MAKE 2)

Rnd 1: in A, dc 5 in magic ring; or ch 2, dc 5 in 2nd ch from hook. (5 sts)

Rnd 2: (2dc in each st) around. (10 sts)

Rnd 3: dc 1, 2dc in next st, dc 1, 2dc in next st, htr 1, (tr 1, picot, tr 1) in next st, htr 1, 2dc in next st, dc 1, 2dc in next st. (16 sts)

Fasten off and sew to top of Head.

> *To make a picot stitch, see Edgings and Embellishments: Picot Edging. For changing colour in amigurumi, see Troubleshooting: The Jogless Join.*

LEGS (MAKE 4)

Stuff with toy filling as the parts take shape.

Rnd 1: in D, dc 4 in magic ring; or ch 2, dc 4 in 2nd ch from hook. (4 sts)

Rnd 2: (2dc in each st) around. (8 sts)

Rnds 3–4: dc 1 in each st around.

Rnd 5: in A, (dc 1, 2dc in next st) around. (12 sts)

Rnds 6–13: dc 1 in each st around.

Fasten off and sew to Body.

BLANKET

In G, ch 13.

Row 1: dc 1 in 2nd ch from hook, dc 1 in each st across, turn. (12 sts)

Row 2: ch 1, dc 1 in each st to end, turn.

Rows 3–4: in F, rep **Row 1**.

Rows 5–6: in B, rep **Row 1**.

Rows 7–30: in E, rep **Row 1**.

Rows 31–32: in B, rep **Row 1**.

Rows 33–34: in F, rep **Row 1**.

Rows 35–36: in G, rep **Row 1**.

Fasten off and stitch to body.

> *Sewing body parts together may put a crocheter off making amigurumi items, but it's not as difficult as it seems, and you don't need to be an expert at sewing either. Thread a tapestry needle with the yarn end and hold (or pin) the body part in place. Sew around the piece, working through the inside (back) loops of the final round of stitches and catching a corresponding stitch from the main part until it is firmly secured (B).*

BASKETS (MAKE 2)

Rnd 1: in C, dc 6 in magic ring; or ch 2, dc 6 in 2nd ch from hook. (6 sts)

Rnd 2: (2dc in each st) around. (12 sts)

Rnd 3: (dc 1, 2dc in next st) around. (18 sts)

Rnd 4: (dc 2, 2dc in next st) around. (24 sts)

Rnd 5: (dc 3, 2dc in next st) around. (30 sts)

Rnds 6–10: dc 1 in each st around.

Rnd 11: dc 1, ch 7, sk 3 sts, dc 1 in each st around. (27 sts, 7 ch)

Rnd 12: dc 1, dc 7 in 7ch-sp, dc 1 in each st around. (34 sts)

Fasten off and weave in ends (see Troubleshooting: Weaving in Ends).

To decorate, use B to add surface crochet (see Modern Techniques: Surface Crochet) between **Rnds 7 and 8** and **Rnds 9 and 10**.

BASKET STRAP

Leave a 15cm (6in) tail at the beginning and end for sewing to the baskets.

In C, ch 4.

Row 1: dc 1 in 2nd ch from hook, dc 1, turn. (3 sts)

Rows 2–16: ch 1, dc 1 in each st to end, turn.

Fasten off.

Sew a Basket to each end, then stitch securely to Body.

HARNESS

In F, make enough ch to fit around the Muzzle and back of the Head. Stitch in place.

PICOT GARLANDS (MAKE 2)

In F (G), ch 4, *picot, ch 4; rep from * to go around neck and chest.

Stitch Garlands to Body.

EAR TASSELS (MAKE 2)

For each Ear, cut 1 strand approx 15cm (6in) in each of F and G, fold in half together and loop through top of Ear to make a tassel (see Edgings and Embellishments: Tassels). Trim to equal lengths.

TUNISIAN CROCHET

The Tunisian technique is a very different method of crochet; it uses a longer hook, often with a stopper at the end, to pick up all the stitches in one row (the forward pass) and then release them on the following row (the return pass), all without turning your work. This places this Tunisian style somewhere between knitting and crochet, and requires a slight change in how you hold and manoeuvre the hook and yarn. In this crochet method, stitches are linked both horizontally and vertically, creating a fairly firm fabric with slightly less stretch than regular crochet – but this way of working can, of course, be used for a huge range of projects, including blankets, cushions, clothes and accessories.

CASTING ON

Tunisian crochet benefits from using a slightly larger hook size than you would do usually – this gives you the space to twist your hook and create the stitches. There are three Tunisian crochet stitches that follow (simple, knit and purl) and all are cast on in exactly the same manner each time, so follow this method at the start of a pattern.

1. To create the cast on, make a foundation chain with the correct number of stitches. For the first forward pass, you'll work back across the chain – the best way to get a neat edge is to turn your chain and work through the back 'bump' of the stitch: insert the hook into the second bump after your hook (ignoring the chain just completed), yarn over (A) and draw up a loop (2 loops on hook) (B).

2. Insert the hook into the next bump (C), yarn over and draw up another loop (3 loops on hook) (D). Continue across the chain in the same way to the end of the row. You'll have all the stitches on your hook and are ready to complete the return pass.

3. For the return pass: ch 1 (unlike regular crochet, the turning chain here is made at the end of a row). Yarn over and draw it through the first 2 loops (E).

4. Yarn over and draw it through the next 2 loops. Repeat this process until you have taken all but the last stitch off your hook (1 loop on hook) (F).

You have now cast on your stitches and completed a return row, so you're ready to start the Tunisian pattern of your choice.

Due to the way it is created, Tunisian crochet often curls while you are working with it – but is easily solved with blocking afterwards (see Finishing Up: Blocking).

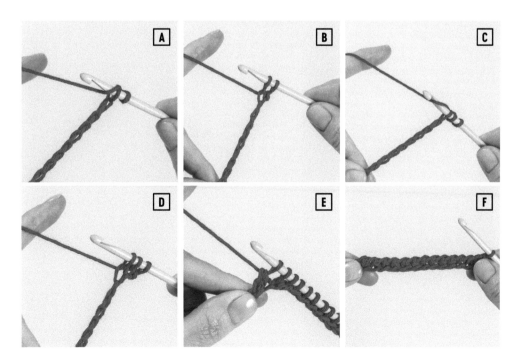

TUNISIAN SIMPLE STITCH

This stitch is exactly as it sounds – it's the simplest Tunisian crochet stitch. To make the first row, you must have already completed the cast on and return pass as described. You'll notice there are vertical bars across the stitches facing you, and it's through these bars that you'll make the stitches.

1. Insert your hook through the first bar to the left of your hook. Yarn over and draw the loop through the stitch (2 loops on hook) (A). Do the same through the next vertical bar (3 loops on hook) (B).

2. Continue to pick up stitches across the row, working through all the vertical bars, until you reach the end of the row. The last stitch is made through the 'V' at the very edge of the piece of crochet (C).

3. When you have finished this forward pass row, work the return pass in the same way as the return pass of the cast on.

SIMPLE STITCH CAST OFF

To cast off the stitches, you need work a forward pass.

1. Insert your hook under the first vertical bar, yarn over and draw the yarn through the vertical bar and the loop on your hook (D).

2. Repeat Step 1 across the row to cast off all the stitches, then fasten off.

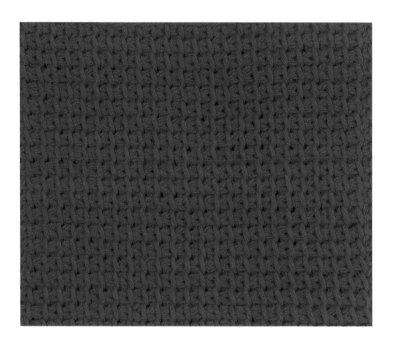

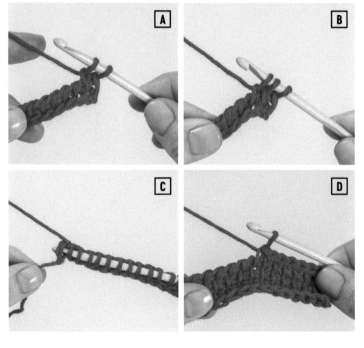

TUNISIAN KNIT STITCH

This stitch resembles stockinette stitch in knitting and produces a thick and soft fabric.

1. Begin in the usual way with a cast on and return pass (E).

2. Next, insert your hook straight through the stitch to the right of the vertical bar from **front** to **back**, yarn over and draw up a loop (F).

3. Repeat Step 3 across the row, making the final stitch through the 'V' at the edge of your crochet (G).

4. Make the standard (cast on) return pass, then repeat these two passes for each row to continue the pattern (H).

KNIT STITCH CAST OFF

As with Tunisian simple stitch, you'll cast off on a forward pass.

1. Insert your hook through the stitch to the right of the vertical bar, yarn over, draw up a loop, yarn over and draw the yarn through both loops (I).

2. Repeat Step 1 across the row to cast off all the stitches, then fasten off.

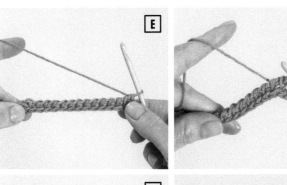

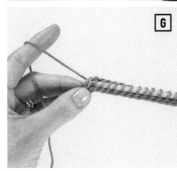

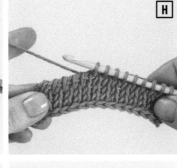

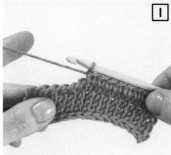

It can sometimes feel a little fiddly, trying to twist your hook while holding all the stitches on it at the same time – you might find it easier to use a slightly longer hook than usual, so that the stitches have more room to slide up and down with ease.

TUNISIAN PURL STITCH

This stitch is a little trickier than the simple or knit stitch, but is worth mastering as the finished piece will resemble an attractive purl stitch on the right side.

1. Make the cast on and return pass as usual, then move the working yarn to the front (A).

2. Insert the hook through the vertical bar (as you would do for simple stitch), yarn over and draw through one loop (B).

3. With the working yarn to the front again, insert your hook under the next vertical bar and continue across the row (C).

4. For the last stitch, return the working yarn to the back, insert the hook through the 'V' at the edge, yarn over and draw up a loop (D).

5. Make the return row in the usual way. Repeat the forward and return passes until your piece is finished.

6. To cast off, use the same method as for simple stitch.

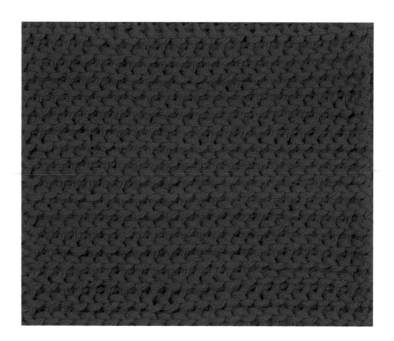

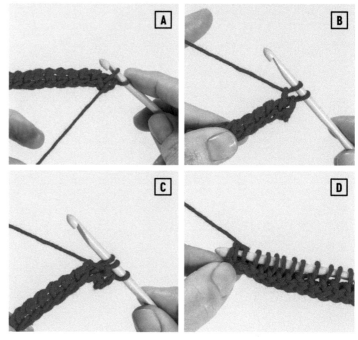

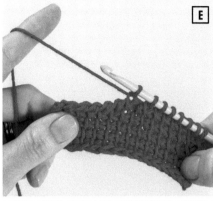

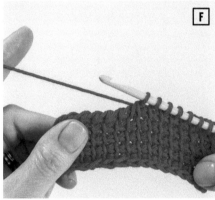

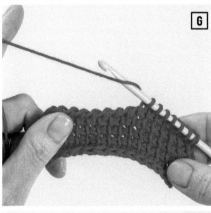

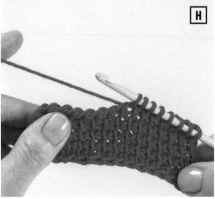

INCREASING AND DECREASING IN TUNISIAN CROCHET

As with all stitches, it's easy to increase and decrease, and there are lots of different methods, depending on which Tunisian stitches you're using and the effect you want to achieve.

A simple way of decreasing is to just skip a stitch when working the forward pass (E). Another method is to crochet 2 stitches together by working through 2 of the vertical bars at the same time on the forward pass (F).

To increase the number of stitches, you can either insert a new stitch on your forward pass by working between the vertical bars and drawing up an extra loop (G), or you can yarn over before working one of the stitches (H), which will also produce an extra stitch.

OMBRÉ PURSE

Worked as a rectangle in Tunisian simple stitch, with a gradual, ombré colour change, this handy little pouch can either be used to store useful hooks and notions or precious items.

I USED

YARN

Rico Essentials Cotton DK (100% Cotton / 50g / 142yds/130m)

+ Yarn A: Red (02); 1 ball
+ Yarn B: Fuchsia (14); 1 ball
+ Yarn C: Lotus (57); 1 ball
+ Yarn D: Azalea (68); 1 ball
+ Yarn E: Pumpkin (87); 1 ball

HOOKS AND ACCESSORIES

+ 5.5mm Tunisian hook
+ Tapestry needle
+ Sewing needle
+ 20cm (8in) zip and matching thread

FINISHED SIZE

18 x 13cm (7 x 5in) approx

YOU COULD USE

Any similar DK cotton yarn and suitable hook to match gauge

TENSION

10 x 10cm (4 x 4in) square: 17 sts and 15 rows (using 5.5mm hook measured over pattern)

To create the colour changes, work with 2 strands at a time (see Multi-strand Ombré Crochet).

PATTERN

Using 2 strands of A, ch 30.

Row 1: forward pass for Tunisian simple stitch, return pass. (30 sts)

Row 2: forward pass, drop 1 strand of A and pick up 1 strand of E, return pass.

Rows 3–4: rep **Rows 1 and 2**, working in 2 strands of E.

Rows 5–6: rep **Rows 1 and 2**, working in 1 strand of E and 1 strand of D.

Rows 7–8: rep **Rows 1 and 2**, working in 2 strands of D.

Rows 9–10: rep **Rows 1 and 2**, working in 1 strand of D and 1 strand of B.

Rows 11–12: rep **Rows 1 and 2**, working in 2 strands of B.

Rows 13–14: rep **Rows 1 and 2**, working in 1 strand of B and 1 strand of C.

Rows 15–16: rep **Rows 1 and 2**, working in 2 strands of C.

Rows 17–31: rep **Rows 1 and 2**, working backwards through the colour sequence.

Row 32: cast off.

Fasten off and weave in ends (see Troubleshooting: Weaving in Ends).

Place RS together and use whip stitch (see Finishing Up: Joining Motifs and Edges) to join the side edges together. Turn the work.

Pin the zip in place just inside the top opening; hand sew to finish. Add a tassel to the zip pull (see Edgings and Embellishments: Tassels).

TUNISIAN ENTRELAC CROCHET

Entrelac crochet is a textured pattern in which squares of Tunisian simple stitch are combined to create a patchwork effect. There are quite a few ways of producing entrelac – squares can be created around a central starting point, or a long foundation chain can be used as a base for the pattern to be created in horizontal rows. In this sample, the squares are worked with four yarn colours in such a way as to create diagonals.

As each square consists of just a few stitches, this technique can be worked with a regular hook; work your chain and slip stitches loosely, so that you can make new stitches into them easily.

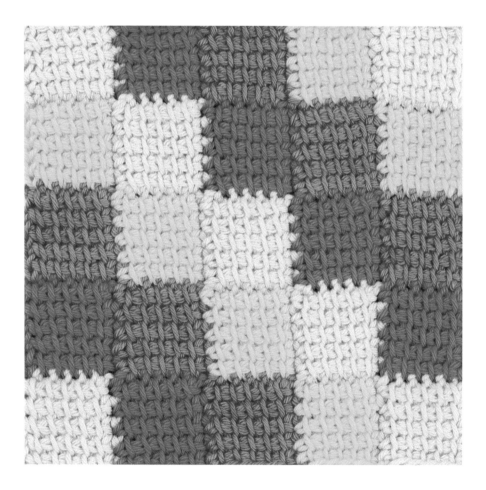

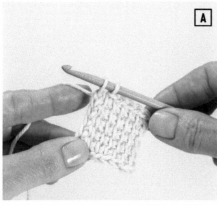

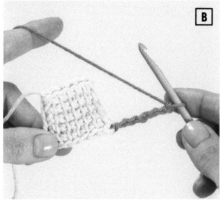

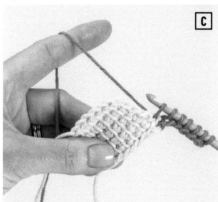

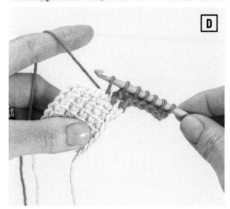

MAKING DIAGONAL TUNISIAN ENTRELAC

SQUARE 1

In A, ch 7.

Make forward pass with Tunisian simple stitch (7 loops on hook), then the return pass.

Repeat last row 4 more times.

Cast off as for Tunisian simple stitch (A).

SQUARE 2

Join B to the bottom-right corner of the previous square, ch 6 (B).

For the forward pass, pick up 5 loops from the chain (6 loops on hook), then draw up the last loop from the corresponding stitch at the side of the next square (7 loops on hook) (C). Make the return pass, but do not ch 1 at the beginning.

For the next forward pass, repeat the last row (D). Again, when making the return pass, do not ch 1 at the beginning.

Repeat the last row 3 more times.

Cast off, making final stitch in the same stitch as the beginning of the last return pass (E).

SQUARE 3

In B, working in the forward pass stitches across the top of the square to the left, pick up 6 loops. (7 loops on hook) (F). Return pass.

Repeat the last row 4 more times.

Cast off (G).

SQUARE 4

In C, repeat **Square 2**.

SQUARE 5

In C, working in the forward pass stitches across the top of the square to the left, pick up 5 loops (6 loops on hook), then draw up the last loop from the corresponding stitch at the side of the next square (7 loops on hook) (H). Make the return pass.

On the next forward pass, pick up 5 loops (6 loops on hook), then draw up the last loop from the corresponding stitch at the side of the next square (7 loops on hook). Return pass.

Repeat the last row 3 more times.

Cast off.

REMAINING SQUARES

Work pattern as follows (see also chart, right):

Square 6 in C, repeat **Square 3**.

Square 7 in D, repeat **Square 2**.

Squares 8 and 9 in D, repeat **Square 5**.

Square 10 in D, repeat **Square 3**.

Square 11 in A, repeat **Square 2**.

Squares 12 to 14 in A, repeat **Square 5**.

Square 15 in A, repeat **Square 3**.

Squares 16 to 18 in B, repeat **Square 5**.

Square 19 in B, repeat **Square 3**.

Squares 20 and 21 in C, repeat **Square 5**.

Square 22 in C, repeat **Square 3**.

Square 23 in D, repeat **Square 5**.

Square 24 in D, repeat **Square 3**.

Square 25 in A, repeat **Square 5**.

DIAGONAL TUNISIAN ENTRELAC CHART

15	19	22	24	25
10	14	18	21	23
6	9	13	17	20
3	5	8	12	16
1	2	4	7	11

FREE-FORM CROCHET

Free-form crochet is the art of not following a pattern and instead following the desires of your creative mind – often referred to as 'painting with yarn'. Many of these designs resemble those found in nature, such as spirals and shells, corals and creatures. This is a playful, modern technique that can be used to create sculptural 2D or 3D pieces as show-cased in avant-garde garments and textile artistry. The great thing about free-form crochet is there's no right or wrong – experiment with whatever variations of stitches you like with any yarn you please, and enjoy the liberating experience of unfettered design. To create your own free-form piece, why not attempt a small-scale project like a simple brooch or embellish an exisitng item?

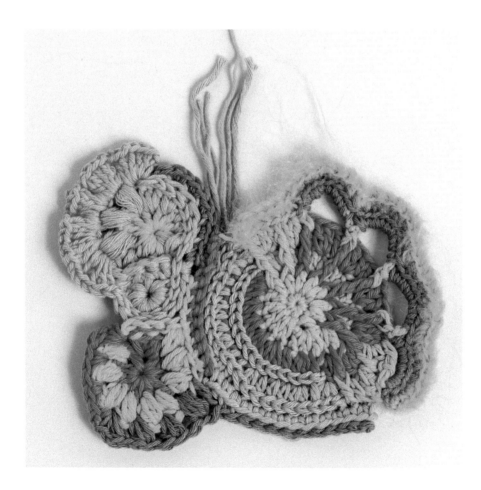

SOME FREE-FORM TERMS AND TECHNIQUES

SCRUMBLING

This refers to the technique of crocheting several pieces and joining them together to create the finished work, so there's no need to worry about getting it right from the off – make different pieces and play with their arrangement to see what you like.

CIRCLES AND SPIRALS (A)

Begin with making several stitches into a magic ring, working each round as you please, and increasing the number or height of your stitches to create an interesting shape. Don't worry about counting the stitches, just do what works.

RUFFLES (B)

These are easy. Simply make lots of stitches into one stitch and repeat around a circle or across a row. The additional stitches will create ruffles as they jostle for space.

CHAIN STITCHES (C)

You'll find these are handy for creating arcs and spaces in your work. Use them to anchor stitches, or join up parts of your project – and you can, of course, work over or into them with more stitches.

EDGING (D)

Create more defined borders to your shapes by edging them in a contrasting colour or a textured yarn.

ENDS (E)

Unlike other projects, messy ends can be a feature. You can always sew them in, as you would do any other project, but there's nothing to stop you simply knotting them together and snipping them off at the back, or leaving them loose to add interest.

DECORATIVE STITCHES (F)

Create texture in your project by using a variety of stitches. Why not try bobbles, post stitches, surface crochet, ripples, tall and short stitches? Enjoy breaking the rules!

TAPESTRY CROCHET

Tapestry crochet is a colourwork technique found across the globe, where it is used to make hats, bags and homewares in an array of stunning, often geometric, patterns. Some are simple, with just one colour change, while others have many colours and complicated, intricate designs.

In this technique, charts are used to show colours and pattern repeats. More than one colour is worked in each row or round, with the unused yarns being carried along and crocheted over to make them almost invisible – as you can just see in the sample below. Usually, compact double crochet stitches (see Basic Stitches: Double Crochet) are used, as these are dense enough to hide the other colours and add stability to the finished piece, but taller stitches can be utilised, too.

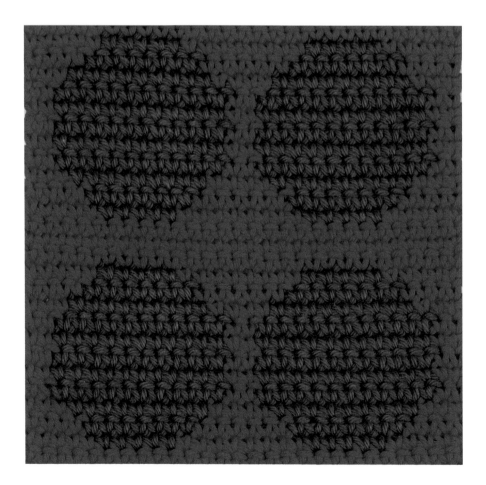

FOLLOWING A CHART WHEN WORKING IN ROWS

The chart for a pattern worked in rows is read from the bottom up, with Row 1 (and all odd-numbered rows) being read from right to left. Row 2 (and all even-numbered rows) are read from left to right.

FOLLOWING A CHART WHEN WORKING IN ROUNDS

If you are given a short pattern-repeat chart for working in the round, just read the chart from right to left and repeat for the whole round. Be aware that stitches tend to shift to the right slightly on successive rounds when crocheting in the round in this technique (see chart, right).

Other charts are depicted in the round and are just as easy as following a chart in rows. You'll find the beginning of each round marked with its number, and you'll need to read each round in an anti-clockwise direction (unless told otherwise). The circular chart will show you where the stitches, increases and colour changes are made.

SAMPLE TAPESTRY STITCH CHART

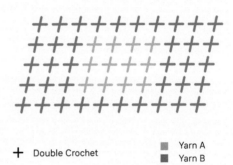

+ Double Crochet

■ Yarn A
■ Yarn B

New colours can be picked up wherever they are needed and are dropped as soon as they have been finished with. Sometimes, it's easier to do this than carry them under great lengths of stitches.

Mostly, only two or three colours are carried at any one time, otherwise the fabric can become dense and it's more difficult to conceal the carried yarn under the stitches.

TAPESTRY CROCHET COLOUR CHART

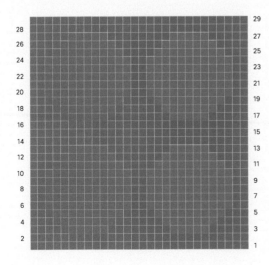

■ Yarn A
■ Yarn B

For this sample, make a foundation ch of 27.

Follow the chart to see where the colour changes need to be made.

Row 1: dc 1 in 2nd ch from hook, dc 1 in each ch across, turn.

Rows 2–26: ch 1, dc 1 in each st across, turn.

MAKING A COLOUR CHANGE

1. On a row or round where there will be a colour change, you need to carry the new colours along, encasing them within the stitches, so that they are ready to use when you need them (A).

2. Making a colour change is quick, and the method is the same regardless of whether you're working in a round or row. Begin the colour change in the previous stitch: in the old colour, make the stitch as usual but, before you make the final yarn over, bring the old colour to the front (this completes the stitch on the reverse side), then pick up and draw through a loop of the new colour (B).

3. Pass the old colour to the back and continue in the new colour, crocheting over the old colour as you go (C).

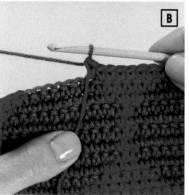

Try to keep your tension fairly tight when working tapestry stitches, as this will help you conceal the unused yarn that you are crocheting over. You might find that a smaller hook size helps with this, too.

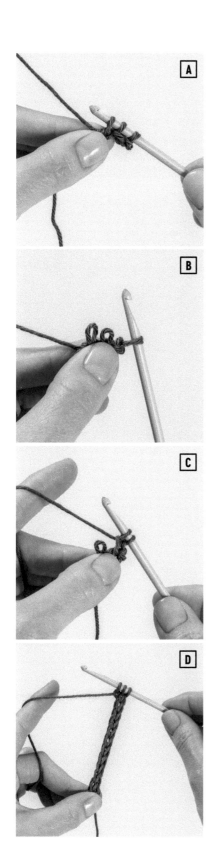

MAKING AN I-CORD

Originally invented as a knitted cord, you can easily crochet one, too. It is a little fiddly at first, but do persevere as it takes a few rows for the cord to form. If you're having trouble holding onto the loose loops, you might want to use a slightly bigger hook.

1. Ch 3, then insert your hook into the 2nd ch from the hook, yarn over and draw up a loop. Insert your hook into the last ch, yarn over and draw up a loop (3 loops on hook) (A).

2. Take your hook out of the last two loops and pinch hold of them – you don't want them to unravel when you work the next step (B).

3. Yarn over and draw up a loop (1 loop on hook), then insert your hook into the next loop, yarn over and draw up a loop (2 loops on hook) (C).

4. Insert your hook into the last loop, yarn over and draw up a loop (3 loops on hook). Repeat from Step 2 until your i-cord is as long as you need it (D).

5. To finish, yarn over and draw through all 3 loops.

Fasten off.

> *The 'i' is said to stand for 'idiot'. Idiot-proof or because an idiot didn't turn their knitting needles? You decide...*

MOCHILA STYLE BAG

The Wayuu people of Columbia produce magnificent handmade bags using incredible geometric patterns. One of the most enduring designs is a small bag with a circular base and drawstring closure in tapestry crochet.

I USED

YARN

Stylecraft Classique Cotton DK
(100% Cotton / 50g / 100yds/92m)

+ Yarn A: White (3660); 1 ball
+ Yarn B: Peppermint (3691); 1 ball
+ Yarn C: Fuchsia (3692); 1 ball

Erika Knight Gossypium Cotton
(100% Cotton / 50g / 109yds/100m)

+ Yarn D: Mouse (502); 1 ball

NEEDLES AND ACCESSORIES

+ 3.5mm hook
+ Stitch marker
+ Tapestry needle

FINISHED SIZE

17 x 17cm (6½ x 6½in) square

YOU COULD USE

Any similar DK cotton yarn and
suitable hook

TENSION

Not essential to this project

> *To keep the project manageable, this
> design mostly uses two colours when
> colour changing is needed. For each
> round, simply carry the unused yarn
> around under your stitches, so it's ready
> to be used when you next need it.*

This bag is crocheted in one piece, starting
with the base and working up the sides in
continuous rounds. Use a stitch marker to
mark the first stitch of each round.

PATTERN

Letter preceding stitch indicates yarn colour for
this and following stitches, until the next letter.

Rnd 1: C: ch 2, 6dc in 2nd ch from hook. (6 sts)

Work in BLO for rest of pattern.

Rnd 2: (2dc in each st) around. (12 sts)

Rnd 3: (C: dc 1, B: dc 1 in same st) around. (24 sts)

Rnd 4: (C: dc 1, B: 2dc in next st) around. (36 sts)

Rnd 5: (C: dc 1, B: 2dc in next st, dc 1) around.
(48 sts)

Rnd 6: (C: dc 1, B: dc 3) around.

Rnd 7: (C: dc 1, B: 2dc in next st, dc 2) around.
(60 sts)

Rnd 8: (C: dc 1, B: 2dc in next st, dc 3) around.
(72 sts)

STITCH CHART FOR BAG BASE

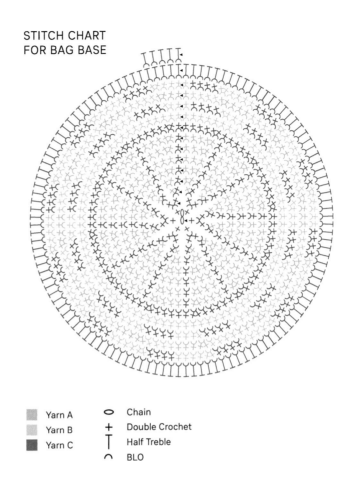

	Yarn A		$\circ$	Chain
	Yarn B		$+$	Double Crochet
	Yarn C		T	Half Treble
			$\cap$	BLO

Rnd 9: C: dc 1, *2dc in next st, dc 5; rep from * until 5 sts remaining, 2dc in next st, dc 4. (84 sts)

Rnd 10: A: dc 1 in each st around.

Rnd 11: A: dc 1, 2dc in next st, *C: dc 4, A: dc 2, 2dc in next st; rep from * until 5 sts remaining, C: dc 4, A: dc 1. (96 sts)

Rnd 12: A: dc 2, 2dc in next st, dc 4, *B: dc 3, 2dc in next st, A: dc 4; rep from * until one st remaining, B: dc 1. (108 sts)

Rnd 13: B: dc 4, A: dc 1 in same st as previous st, dc 8, 2dc in next st, C: dc 4, *A: dc 4, 2dc in next st, C: dc 4; rep from * until one st remaining, A: dc 1. (120 sts)

Rnd 14: A: htr 5, C: htr 1 in each st around.

Rnd 15 (short round): C: htr 5, leave 115 sts unworked.

SIDES

For **all** rnds, work dc 1 BLO in each st around.

To follow the chart for colour changes in the 12-stitch pattern repeat see From Colour Chart; or for complete written instructions see With Colour Changes.

FROM COLOUR CHART

Rnd 16: C: dc 1 in each st around.

Refer to chart for colour changes.

Rnds 17–42: dc 1 in each st around.

Rnd 43: A: dc 1 in each st around.

Rnd 44: A: *dc 9, ch 3, sk 3 sts; rep from * around.

Rnd 45: A: *dc 9, 3dc in 3ch-sp; rep from * around.

Fasten off.

Rnd 46: C: one sl st in each st around.

Fasten off.

WITH COLOUR CHANGES

Letter preceding number indicates yarn colour for number of dc 1 BLO stitches until next letter. If letter only, work all stitches in the round in this colour.

Rnd 16: C: dc 1 in each st around.

Rnd 17: A.

Rnd 18: *D: 5, A: 3, D: 1, A: 3; rep from * around.

Rnd 19: *A: 1, D: 3, A: 3, D: 3, A: 2; rep from * around.

Rnd 20: *A: 2, D: 1, A: 3, D: 5, A: 1; rep from * around.

Rnd 21: A.

COLOUR CHART FOR SIDES

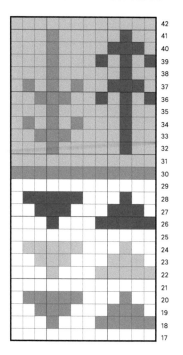

☐	Pattern repeat area
	Yarn A
	Yarn B
	Yarn C
	Yarn D

Rnd 22: *B: 5, A: 3, B: 1, A: 3; rep from * around.

Rnd 23: *A: 1, B: 3, A: 3, B: 3, A: 2; rep from * around.

Rnd 24: *A: 2, B: 1, A: 3, B: 5, A: 1; rep from * around.

Rnd 25: A.

Rnd 26: *C: 5, A: 3, C: 1, A: 3; rep from * around.

Rnd 27: *A: 1, C: 3, A: 3, C: 3, A: 2; rep from * around.

Rnd 28: *A: 2, C: 1, A: 3, C: 5, A: 1; rep from * around.

Rnd 29: A.

Rnd 30: D.

Rnd 31: B.

Rnd 32: *B: 2, C: 1, B: 5, D: 1, B: 3; rep from * around.

Rnd 33: *B: 2, C: 1, B: 4, D: 3, B: 2; rep from * around.

Rnd 34: *B: 2, C: 1, B: 3, D: 1, B: 1, D: 1, B: 1, D: 1, B: 1; rep from * around.

Rnd 35: rep **Rnd 32**.

Rnd 36: *C: 1, B: 1, C: 1, B: 1, C: 1, B: 2, D: 3, B: 2; rep from * around.

Rnd 37: *B: 1, C: 3, B: 2, D: 1, B: 1, D: 1, B: 1, D: 1, B: 1; rep from * around.

Rnd 38: rep **Rnd 32**.

Rnd 39: *C: 1, B: 1, C: 1, B: 1, C: 1, B: 3, D: 1, B: 3; rep from * around.

Rnd 40: *B: 1, C: 3, B: 4, D: 1, B: 3; rep from * around.

Rnd 41: *B: 2, C: 1, B: 5, D: 1, B: 3; rep from * around.

Rnd 42: B.

Rnd 43: A.

Rnd 44: A: *dc 9, ch 3, sk 3 sts; rep from * around.

Rnd 45: A: *dc 9, 3dc in 3ch-sp; rep from * around.

Fasten off.

Rnd 46: C: one sl st in each st around.

Fasten off.

In D, make an i-cord approx 50cm (20in) long (see Tapestry Crochet: Making an I-Cord).

> *To give the strap the same patterning as the bag, you'll need to fasten off at the end of each row and begin from the right edge each time. Do not turn your work so RS is always facing you. The strap pattern is based on a 6-stitch repeat, so if you want to adjust the length, simply ensure your foundation chain is a multiple of 6.*

STRAP

To follow the chart for colour changes follow From Colour Chart above; or for complete written instructions see With Colour Changes. From Row 2 work in BLO for **all** rows.

In C, ch 168.

FROM CHART

Row 1: ch 1, dc 1 in 2nd ch from hook, dc 1 in each st across. (168 sts)

Refer to chart for colour changes.

Rows 2–4: dc 1 in each st across.

Row 5: C: htr 1 in each st across.

WITH COLOUR CHANGES

Row 1: ch 1, dc 1 in 2nd ch from hook, dc 1 in each st across. (168 sts)

Row 2: *B: 3, A: 3; rep from * across.

Row 3: *B: 1, D: 1, B: 2, D: 1, B: 1; rep from * across.

Row 4: *A: 3, B: 3; rep from * across.

Row 5: C: htr 1 in each st across.

TO MAKE UP

Stitch the strap to the inside of the Bag, then thread the i-cord through the chain spaces. Make 2 tassels (see Edgings and Embellishments: Tassels) from leftover yarn, and secure to the ends of the i-cord. Weave in all ends (see Troubleshooting: Weaving in Ends).

COLOUR CHART FOR STRAP

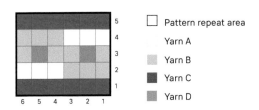

☐ Pattern repeat area

Yarn A

Yarn B

Yarn C

Yarn D

MODERN GRANNIES

What's not to love about a granny square? These traditional motifs, made in the main from clusters of trebles, have stood the test of time and are as popular today for the modern crocheter as they ever have been. There are thousands of different versions of this emblematic square, some using a mix of different stitches, others varying the ways that colours or yarns are combined – and some don't even start off as a square.

THE VERSATILE GRANNY SQUARE

These beauties can be created to suit your own style and varied as much or as little as you like. Why not change the size and make lots of small, two-round granny squares joined together to create a scarf? Or keep crocheting and crocheting until you've made hundreds of rounds – and an enormous blanket? And what about yarn choice? You could design a delicate wrap using squares of mohair or sock yarn, or crochet a giant wall hanging with super-size yarn. And don't forget colour choice is important, too – experiment with changing colour every round, or every square, or just let the pattern provide the interest.

Things to try... The chart on the next page uses a ch 1 between each treble cluster, but some crocheters prefer the look of their squares without it – it's up to you.

Sometimes, granny squares appear to spiral as they're worked, and this can be particularly noticeable when making larger squares. One method to stop this completely is to turn your square over after every round and work back in the opposite direction.

If you are working rounds of different colour, the neatest way to start and finish your round is with a standing stitch and ch 1 at the beginning, and invisible fastening off at the end (see Troubleshooting: Invisible Fastening Off).

MAKING A CLASSIC GRANNY SQUARE

Ch 4, join with a sl st to make a ring.

Rnd 1: ch 3 (counts as first tr), all into ring: 2tr, ch 2, *3tr, ch 2; rep from * twice more, join with a sl st to top of 3ch. (12 tr, 8 ch)

Rnd 2: sl st across to 2ch-sp, (ch 3 [counts as 1tr throughout], 2tr in next st, ch 2, 3tr) in same 2ch-sp, ch 1, *(3tr, ch 2, 3tr) in next 2ch-sp, ch 1; rep from * twice more, join with a sl st to top of 3ch. (24 tr, 12 ch)

Rnd 3: sl st across to 2ch-sp, (ch 3, 2tr, ch 2, 3tr) in same 2ch-sp, ch 1, *3tr, ch 1 in 1ch-sp, (3tr, ch 2, 3tr) in 2ch-sp, ch 1; rep from * twice more, 3tr, ch 1 in 1ch-sp, join with a sl st to top of 3ch. (36 tr, 16 ch)

Rnds 4 onwards: sl st across to 2ch-sp, (ch 3, 2tr, ch 2, 3tr) in same 2ch-sp, ch 1, *(3tr, ch 1) in each 1ch-sp to corner, (3tr, ch 2, 3tr) in 2ch-sp, ch 1; rep from * twice more, 3tr, ch 1 in each 1ch-sp to corner, join with a sl st to top of 3ch.

CLASSIC GRANNY SQUARE CHART

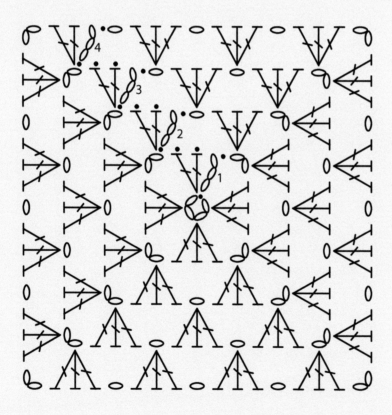

- Slip stitch
- Chain
- Treble

MAKING A CIRCLE GRANNY SQUARE

This sample of the granny square uses a solid circle centre which is squared up into a traditional granny for the final rounds. Work all odd-numbered rounds in Yarn A and all even-numbered rounds in Yarn B.

Rnd 1: ch 4 (counts as 1ch and 1tr), 11tr in 4th ch from hook, join with a sl st to top of 4ch. (12 sts)

Rnds 2-3: ch 3 (counts as 1tr throughout), tr 1 in same st as 3ch, (2tr in each st) around, join with a sl st to top of 3ch. (48 sts)

Rnd 4: ch 3, tr 2, 2tr in next st, *tr 3, 2tr in next st; rep from * around, join with a sl st to top of 3ch. (60 sts)

Rnd 5: ch 3, tr 1, htr 3, dc 2, htr 3, tr 3, (2dtr, ch 2, 2dtr) in next st, *tr 3, htr 3, dc 2, htr 3, tr 3, (2dtr, ch 2, 2dtr) in next st; rep from * twice more, tr 2, join with a sl st to top of 3ch. (72 sts, 8 ch)

Rnd 6: begin in any 2ch-sp, *(ch 3, 2tr, ch 2, 2tr) in 2ch-sp, sk one st, 3tr in next st, (sk 2 sts, 3tr in next st) 5 times, sk one st, *(3tr, ch 2, 3tr) in 2ch-sp, sk one st, 3tr in next st, (sk 2 sts, 3tr in next st) 5 times, sk one st; rep from * around, join with a sl st to top of 3ch. (96 sts, 8 ch)

Rnd 7: begin in any 2ch-sp, (ch 3, 2tr, ch 2, 3tr) in 2ch-sp, ch 1, *3tr in each 1ch-sp to corner, (3tr, ch 2, 3tr) in 2ch-sp; rep from * twice, (3tr, ch 1) in each 1ch-sp to corner, join with a sl st to top of 3ch. (108 sts, 8 ch)

CIRCLE GRANNY SQUARE CHART

- ◠ Chain
- · Slip stitch
- + Double crochet
- ⊤ Half treble
- ⊦ Treble
- ⊦ Double treble
- ◄ Start of round

MODERN LOG CABIN QUILT

Quilting comes right up to date with a play on a dense granny square. Here, it's the strong contrast of colours that create a dazzling, geometric design and a blanket to treasure forever.

I USED

YARN

Stylecraft Wondersoft Merry Go Round DK (100% Acrylic / 100g / 322yds/294m)

+ Yarn A: Stardust (3145); 6 balls
Stylecraft Special DK (100% Acrylic / 100g / 322yds /294m)

+ Yarn B: White (1001); 5 balls
+ Yarn C: Graphite (1063); 5 balls

HOOKS AND ACCESSORIES

+ 4mm hook
+ Tapestry needle

FINISHED SIZE

126 x 130cm (49½ x 51in) approx

YOU COULD USE

Any similar DK acrylic or wool yarn and suitable hook

TENSION

10 x 10cm (4 x 4in) square: 17 sts and 9 rows (using 4mm hook measured over pattern)

LOG CABIN GRANNY SQUARE CHART

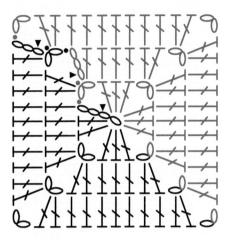

⌒ Chain	■ Yarn A
• Slip stitch	▨ Yarn B or C
┬ Treble	
◄ Start of round	

CHANGING COLOUR MID-ROUND

For this pattern to work, the colours change halfway through the round, at the corner. To change colour from Yarn A (to B or C), ch 1 in A, then ch 1 in the new colour, and continue – this is on odd-numbered rounds only.

To change colour from Yarn B or C to A, ch 2 in the existing colour, then pull up a length of Yarn A to the same height as a new stitch (from where you left it in the row below), 2tr in the same 2ch-sp, then continue – this is for even-numbered rounds only.

PATTERN FOR ONE SQUARE

The 3ch at beginning of each round counts as 1tr. At the end of every round turn the square over to work in the opposite direction.

You'll need to make 36 squares, 18 as below, then 18 swapping Yarns B and C.

Rnd 1: in A, ch 4 (counts as 1ch and 1tr), make all sts into 4th ch from hook: 2tr, ch 2, 3tr, ch 1, in B, ch 1, 3tr, ch 2, 3tr, ch 2, join with a sl st to 3rd ch of 4ch, turn. (12 tr, 8 ch)

Rnd 2: in C, begin in 2ch-sp just made, (ch 3, tr 1), tr 1 in each st to next 2ch-sp, (2tr, ch 2, 2tr) in 2ch-sp, tr 1 in each st to next 2ch-sp, 2tr in 2ch-sp, ch 2, in A, 2tr in same 2ch-sp, tr 1 in each st to next 2ch-sp, (2tr, ch 2, 2tr) in 2ch-sp, tr 1 in each st to next 2ch-sp, 2tr in 2ch-sp, ch 2, join with a sl st to top of 3ch, turn. (28 tr, 8 ch)

Rnd 3: sl st into 2ch-sp, ch 3, tr 1 in same 2ch-sp, tr 1 in each st to next 2ch-sp, (2tr, ch 2, 2tr) in 2ch-sp, tr 1 in each st to next 2ch-sp, 2tr in 2ch-sp, ch 1, in B, ch 1, 2tr in same 2ch-sp, 1tr in each st to next 2ch-sp, (2tr, ch 2, 2tr) in 2ch-sp, tr 1 in each st to next 2ch-sp, 2tr in 2ch-sp, ch 2, join with a sl st to top of 3ch, turn. (44 tr, 8 ch)

Rnds 4–9: rep **Rnds 2 and 3** three times.

Fasten off and weave in ends (see Troubleshooting: Weaving in Ends).

QUILT LAYOUT CHART

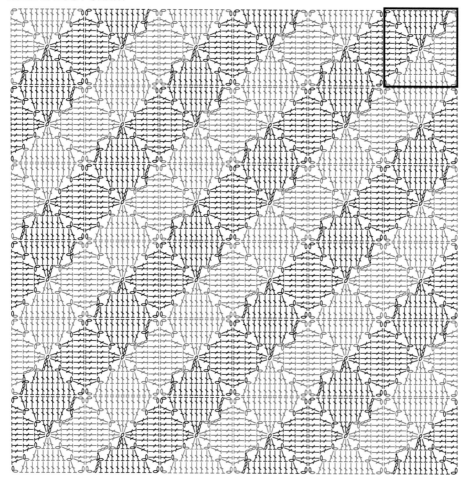

TO MAKE UP

Arrange the squares as shown in the Quilt Layout Chart and join using whip stitch (see Finishing Up: Joining Motifs and Edges).

BORDER

Work with RS facing.

Rnd 1: in B, begin in any 2ch-sp, (ch 3, tr 1, ch 2, 2tr) in 2ch-sp, tr 1 BLO in each st to next 2ch-sp, *(2tr, ch 2, 2tr) in 2ch-sp, tr 1 BLO in each st to 2ch-sp; rep from * around, join with a sl st to top of 3ch.

Rnd 2: in A, begin in any 2ch-sp, *(2dc, ch 2, 2dc) in 2ch-sp, dc 1 in each st to next 2ch-sp; rep from * around, join with a sl st to first dc.

Rnd 3: in C, begin in any 2ch-sp, *(2dc, ch 2, 2dc) in 2ch-sp, dc 1 BLO in each st to next 2ch-sp; rep from * around, join with a sl st to first dc.

Fasten off and weave in ends (see Troubleshooting: Weaving in Ends).

Block the blanket using steam method (see Finishing Up: Blocking).

INTARSIA CROCHET

Intarsia is another form of colourwork, similar in appearance to tapestry crochet. With the tapestry technique, the colours are carried along and crocheted over, encasing them within the stitches, with the result that the work is double-sided. With intarsia, however, unused colours are dropped at the back of the project and then picked back up on the return row, creating definite right and wrong sides, with short floats of yarn between the stitches on the back. Intarsia works particularly well for projects such as cushions, hats and even banners, where the reverse side will not be visible.

READING AN INTARSIA PATTERN

Intarsia colourwork is represented on a grid – it's the easiest way to see where the colour changes need to be made. Follow an intarsia chart, working from right to left for the odd-numbered rows, and left to right for even-numbered ones, with each square representing one stitch.

CHANGING COLOURS

As with most colour changes, the switch to a new colour is made on the final yarn over of the stitch directly before (A and B). When a colour change is needed on the wrong side of the project, ensure the old colour of working yarn is brought to the front (C). This will keep all the floats and yarn ends on the wrong side (D).

MAKING THE INTARSIA SAMPLE

For the foundation chain, in B, ch 14, in A, ch 14.

Follow the chart for colour changes.

Row 1: ch 1, dc 1 2nd ch from hook, dc 1 in each st across, turn. (28 sts)

Rows 2–29: ch 1, dc 1 in each st across, turn. (28 sts)

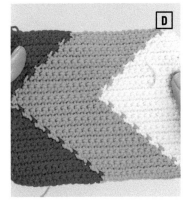

INTARSIA SAMPLE CHART

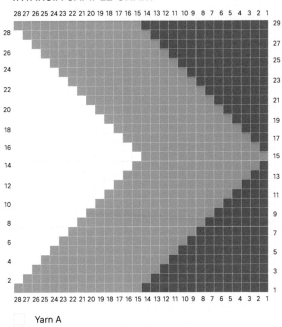

☐ Yarn A
▨ Yarn B
▨ Yarn C

PLAID AND TARTAN

Every winter it seems that tartan makes an appearance in some form or other –
whether it's scarves or kilts – and it's no surprise that we see it in crochet, too.
This popular pattern is based on a traditional Scottish woven fabric and consists
of varying widths of horizontal and vertical bands in multiple colours. Technically,
tartan is an all-over, symmetrical pattern, while plaid is not, but both are easy
to replicate in crochet with a few simple stripes and some surface crochet to
emulate this classic effect.

MAKING CROCHET PLAID AND TARTAN

In the sample here, the horizontal bands are crocheted in rows of double crochet (A), then the vertical stripes are added afterwards using surface crochet (see Modern Techniques: Surface Crochet) (B).

Read the Grid below as you would most other crochet grids, working from right to left for the odd-numbered rows, and left to right for the even-numbered ones.

PLAID AND TARTAN SAMPLE GRID

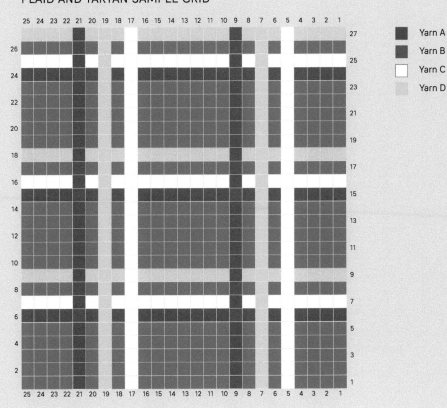

Yarn A
Yarn B
Yarn C
Yarn D

CROCHETING OVER CORD

When crochet stitches are worked over a thicker material base, such as rope, T-shirt yarn or cord, you can create wonderful basketry effects. Use this technique to make all sorts of lovely things for your home or as gifts, including coasters and placemats, bathmats and rugs. This works for projects large or small, so try them tiny or make them huge.

WORKING OVER A CORD

1. Choose a thinner yarn, such as DK, to crochet with and begin with a slip knot on your hook. Swing the hook under the cord to pull up a loop. Yarn over above the cord to complete the first double crochet stitch. Ensure the top 'V' of the stitch will be along the top edge of the cord. Continue to make a few of these wrap double crochet stitches near the end of the cord (A).

2. Start to spiral the cord, making your next crochet stitches into the top of those at the beginning (B).

3. Continue around, making 2dc in each st. On the next round, only increase 2dc in every alternate stitch (C).

4. Reduce the frequency of your increases on each round as you would for crocheting a regular circle – a basic Guide to Increasing in a Circle is given below – but don't worry too much about stitch count; the most important factor is that your coil stays flat (D).

GUIDE TO INCREASING IN A CIRCLE

There's no hard and fast pattern for working over a cord to make a round base, as it depends on what you are crocheting over and the type of yarn, but the basic formula for increasing stitches for a flat circle is a helpful starting point. Use this as an aid, adding more or fewer stitches as you work to prevent your project from curling up.

In normal crochet, the trick is to make your increases evenly and by the same number of stitches you started the first round with. So, for a starting round of 6 stitches, you would increase every round by 6 more stitches at regular intervals.

After your foundation stitches, the pattern generally looks like this.

Rnd 1: dc 6. (6 sts)

Rnd 2: (2dc in each st) around. (12 sts)

Rnd 3: (dc 1, 2dc in next st) around. (18 sts)

Rnd 4: (dc 2, 2dc in next st) around. (24 sts)

Rnd 5: (dc 3, 2dc in next st) around. (30 sts)

Rnd 6: (dc 4, 2dc in next st) around. (36 sts)

And so on, until the pattern changes.

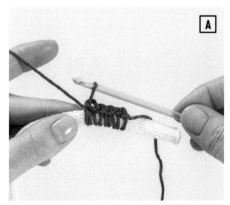

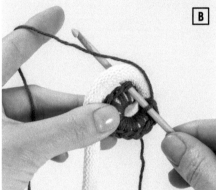

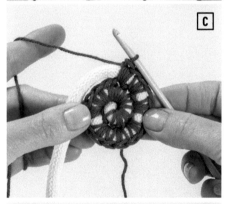

MOROCCAN TILE

The beauty of this motif is that it looks far more complicated than it actually is – and another bonus is that the colours are carried up the sides of the piece, so there are only a few ends to deal with on finishing. In this two-colour technique, you don't necessarily turn for every row; instead first one colour is worked across a row, followed by the second, then the yarns are picked up and worked back the other way on subsequent rows. Perfect for blankets, cushion covers and wearables, too, its versatility is a winner in my book.

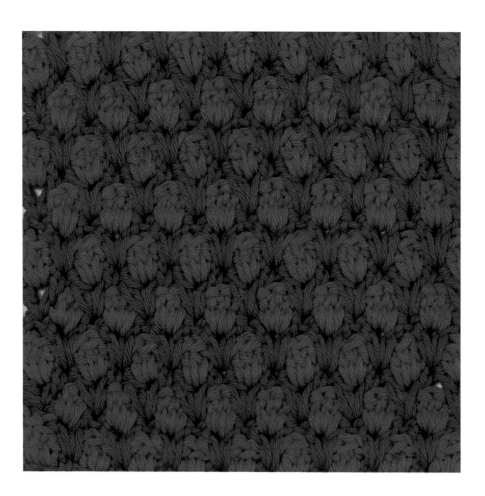

PATTERN

In A, make the foundation chain a multiple of 3, plus 2 more chains.

Row 1: dc 1 in 2nd ch from hook, *ch 2, sk 2 sts, dc 1; rep from * across, ch 3. Remove hook and use a stitch marker to hold final loop. **Do not turn** (A and B).

Row 2: in B and working from right to left, begin in first 2ch-sp, ch 3 (counts as 1tr), 2tr in same sp, (3tr in each 2ch-sp) across. Remove stitch marker from loop of Row 1 and draw A through the loop on hook, turn (C).

Row 3: ch 1, (tr 1, ch 1 , tr 1) in each dc from Rnd 1 until last dc, ch 1, 1 tr. Remove hook and use a stitch marker to hold final loop. **Do not turn** (D and E).

Row 4: insert hook into first 1ch-sp, draw up B (F), ch 3, 2tr in same sp, (3tr in each 1ch-sp) across. Draw A through the loop on hook, turn.

Row 5: ch 2, (tr 1, ch 1, tr 1) in top of first tr from 2 rows below, (tr 1, ch 1, tr 1) in every tr from 2 rows below (directly between the 3tr clusters). Make last tr in top of 2ch from 2 rows below, ch 3. Remove hook and use a stitch marker to hold final loop. **Do not turn**.

Row 6: rep **Row 4**.

Row 7: ch 2, (tr 1, ch 1, tr 1) in every tr from 2 rows below (directly between the 3tr clusters). Make last tr in top of 2ch from 2 rows below, ch 3. Remove hook and use a stitch marker to hold final loop. **Do not turn**.

Rows 8–19: rep **Rows 4, 5, 6, 7** three times.

Fasten off and weave in ends (see Troubleshooting: Weaving in Ends).

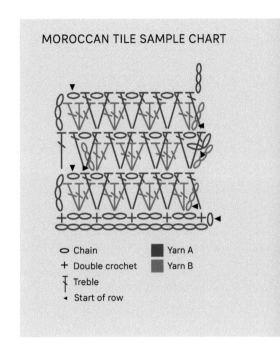

MOROCCAN TILE SAMPLE CHART

◯ Chain
+ Double crochet
⌷ Treble
◀ Start of row

▇ Yarn A
▇ Yarn B

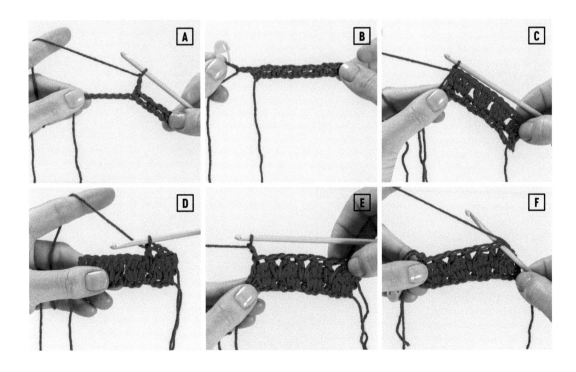

GENERAL TECHNIQUES

I've gathered all the essentials here to help you to finish off your projects, as well as some of my hard-earned suggestions for avoiding crochet catastrophe (believe me, I've been there) in my Troubleshooting section. You're welcome!

EDGINGS AND EMBELLISHMENTS

There's nothing quite like completing your project, stepping back and feeling proud of your accomplishments, is there? Here are a few extras flourishes you might like to add for that special finishing touch.

POMPOM EDGING

This jolly, decorative border is so simple to create. You can vary the chain length and the number of skipped stitches to suit your stitch count.

First, dc 1 to anchor the edging yarn, *ch 6 (A), in the 3rd chain from the hook (tr3tog and ch 1 to close) (B), ch 2, in the bump at the back of the 3rd ch from the hook tr3tog (C and D), sl st in st at the base of the original tr3tog to close the pompom (E and F), ch 3, sk 3 sts, dc 1 in the next st (G and H); repeat from * across.

POMPOM EDGING CHART

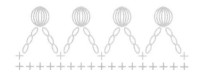

+   Double crochet
o   Chain
◍   Pompom

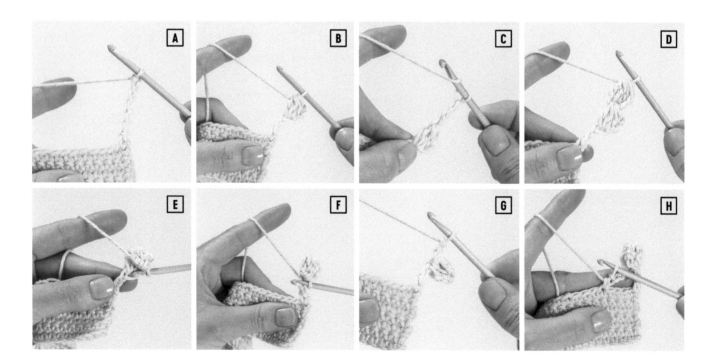

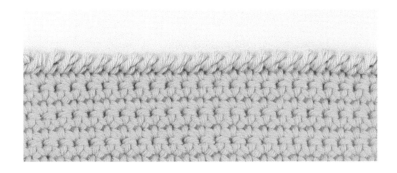

REVERSE DOUBLE CROCHET EDGING

Also known as crab stitch, this neat edging is just a double crochet stitch worked in the opposite direction – from left to right instead of right to left. This creates a wrapped edge for a perfectly understated finish.

First, ch 1 and make the first 'reverse' double crochet in the next stitch along to your **right**, in exactly the same way you would crochet a standard double crochet (A, B and C). This will feel a little awkward to start with, but you'll soon get the hang of handling the yarn and tension. It's always worth having a practice first, so that your stitches look even.

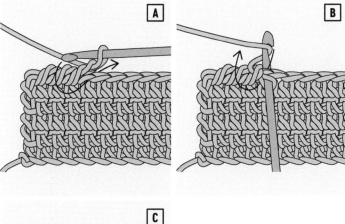

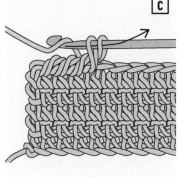

For a solid edging, work into every stitch in the row below; if you prefer a more embroidered effect, try spacing out the crab stitches more.

REVERSE DOUBLE CROCHET EDGING CHART

+   Double crochet

⌣   Crab stitch

PICOT EDGING

A picot stitch is a useful stitch to learn as it adds just a hint of shaping. Picots can be added to the ends of motif shapes (leaves, petals, etc) or, as here, simply to run along as a border on mini points.

To make a picot stitch, ch 3 (D), then make a sl st into the 3rd ch from the hook (E). Continue in double crochet until the next picot is required.

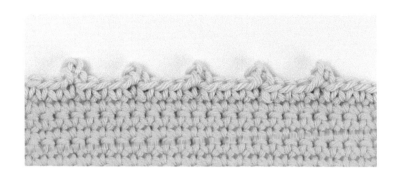

PICOT EDGING CHART

+   Double crochet

🐚   Picot

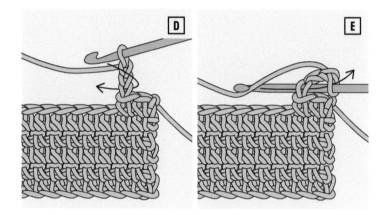

SHELL STITCH EDGING

A pretty, decorative edging is shell stitch, also called fan stitch, where tall stitches are regularly clustered into one stitch and separated by an anchoring stitch. Change the look of the shell by adding more trebles, making chains between the stitches, or even adding picots. This traditional shell pattern works on a multiple of 6 stitches, plus 3 extras.

To begin, dc 1, *sk 2 sts, 5tr in the next st, sk 2 sts, dc 1 in next st; repeat from * across.

SHELL EDGING CHART

+   Double crochet

🔱   5 treble shell

TASSELS

Tassels are a wonderful addition to so many projects and are also a great way of using up those odds and ends of yarn.

1. To start, cut two 30cm (12in) lengths of yarn and set them aside.

2. Wind the yarn around a solid object, like a book or strong card that is twice the desired length of the finished tassel. The more wraps you make, the chunkier your tassel will be.

3. Next, ease the wraps off the object and, using one end, tie the wraps together securely around the middle.

4. Fold the wraps in half, and wind the end of yarn around the top to create the 'head' of the tassel, tying the ends to secure.

5. Cut the loops of yarn and trim for a neat finish.

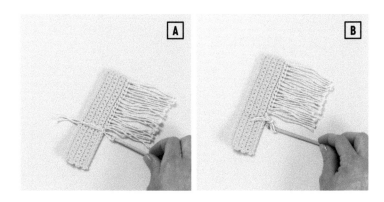

FRINGING

This is great way to finish the edges of projects and can be used on scarves, blankets, and clothing for that swishy, boho vibe.

1. Similar to making a tassel, you'll need to wind lengths of yarn around a book or strong card, but this time the object should be the desired length of the fringe.

2. Wrap as many lengths as you need, and cut at one end only. Remove the card, keeping the fold in the middle of the strands.

3. To attach to the project, use your hook to draw the folded middle of a strand through a stitch at the edge of your project, making a short loop (A). Remove your hook and pull the ends through the loop, then tighten to secure (B). Repeat evenly along the stitches.

POMPOMS

Whether you're making a single pompom to add to a hat or several to decorate the edges of a blanket, pompoms are just fun to make. You can buy pompom makers, which make the whole process quick and easy, but if you fancy the old-school method, try this.

1. On stiff cardboard, use a pair of compasses or draw around something circular to mark the outside edge of your pompom, then draw a smaller circle within the bigger one.

2. Cut out the doughnut shape, then make another so you have a matching pair.

3. Cut long lengths of yarn and, with the pieces of cardboard together, weave the yarn evenly over the sides of the doughnut (C).

4. Keep going, until you can't fit any more yarn through the centre.

5. Insert a sharp pair of scissors between the cardboard pieces and use this channel as a guide to snip through all the yarn (D).

6. Slide a length of yarn between the two cardboard shapes and knot tightly to secure all the strands; leave fairly long yarn tails so that you can attach or hang the pompom (E).

7. Carefully remove the card doughnuts, then neaten up your pompom shape with scissors.

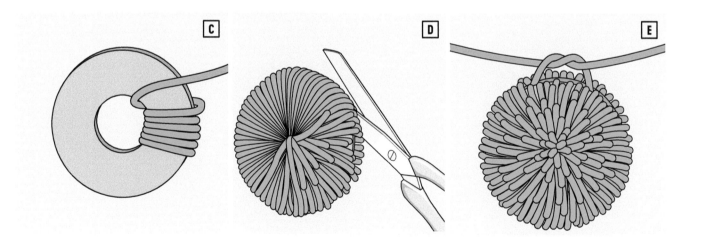

EMBELLISHMENTS

These motifs can be used in so many ways, large or small – as appliqué patches, in garlands, to decorate greeting cards, bookmarks, whatever you wish – and are a useful addition to your repertoire. Follow the charts or the patterns below, and try 4-ply yarn for tiny, delicate versions, or take them to the max in super-size acrylic – you choose.

HEART

Rnd 1: ch 3, all in the 3rd ch from the hook: 2tr, dc 1, 3tr, 2htr, tr 1, 2htr, join with a sl st to top of 3ch. (12 sts)

Rnd 2: ch 3, tr 1 in same st, 2tr in next st, (2tr, htr 1) in next st, 1 spike st into centre hole, (htr 1, 2tr) in next st, (2tr in next st) 4 times, (tr 1, dtr 1, tr 1) in next st, (2tr in next st) twice, join with a sl st to top of 3ch. (26 sts)

Fasten off and weave in ends (see Troubleshooting: Weaving in Ends).

STAR

Rnd 1: ch 3, htr 10 in 3rd ch from hook, join with a sl st to first htr. (10 sts)

Rnd 2: ch 1, *(dc 1, htr 1, tr 1) in first st, ch 2, (tr 1, htr 1, dc 1) in next st; rep from * around, join with a sl st to first dc. (30 sts, 10 ch)

Fasten off and weave in ends (see Troubleshooting: Weaving in Ends).

Block around the 2ch-sp to make the points (see Finishing Up: Blocking).

HEART CHART

	Symbol	Stitch
	⌒	Chain
	•	Slip stitch
	+	Double crochet
	T	Half treble
	⊥	Treble
		Double treble
		Spike double crochet
	◂	Start of round

STAR CHART

	Symbol	Stitch
	⌒	Chain
	•	Slip stitch
	+	Double crochet
	T	Half treble
		Treble
	◂	Start of round

TROUBLESHOOTING

Whether you're halfway through your project, or only just started, here's a few tips and tricks to keep your crochet hooking going smoothly.

THE JOGLESS JOIN

This technique is useful for changing colour when working in the round in amigurumi; because the stitches are worked in a continuous spiral, joining a new colour can leave you with a very visible 'step'. Here's a good way to minimise the difference.

As usual, you'll make the colour change at the last yarn over of the stitch before. With the new yarn on your hook, work the first stitch as a slip stitch, then continue with the pattern. On the next round, work into the slip stitch as a normal stitch. This shallow slip stitch lowers the height of the colour change at this point, making it less noticeable.

CHAINLESS FOUNDATION STITCH

When you're starting a particularly large-scale project, making a long foundation chain can be arduous – and it's easy to make mistakes. A chainless foundation does the work of a chain, combined with the first row of stitches. The twin benefits of this are that it creates a neat and sturdy edge with a consistent tension, and it's quicker than working a foundation chain and Row 1. The steps below demonstrate the chainless foundation stitch for double crochet, but you can also use this chainless method for taller stitches.

1. With a slip knot on your hook, ch 2, insert your hook into the 2nd chain from your hook, *draw the yarn through (2 loops on hook) (A and B).

2. Yarn over and draw it through the first loop to create the first mock chain (2 loops on hook) (C).

3. Yarn over and draw it through both loops, to add the first stitch.

4. For subsequent stitches, insert your hook into the mock chain and repeat from * for as many stitches as needed for your Row 1 (D).

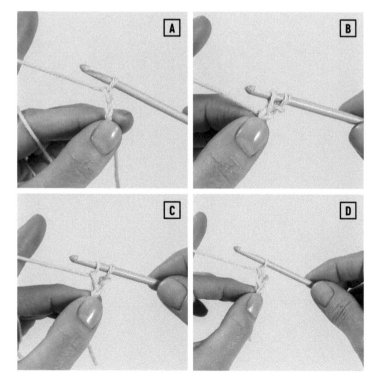

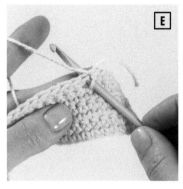

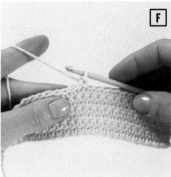

STANDING STITCH

To make your project look a little neater, a standing stitch is a useful way to start a row or round in double crochet, as it removes the need for a slip stitch and ch 1. If you are working with taller stitches, simply make a standing stitch and then ch 1 or 2 to imitate the height of the surrounding stitches.

1. To make the standing stitch, begin with a slip knot on your hook and insert it into the stitch (E).

2. Yarn over and draw the yarn through the stitch (2 loops on hook), yarn over and draw the yarn through both loops to complete the stitch (F).

The standing stitch is very useful when combined with an invisible fastening off (see below) if you are working in the round.

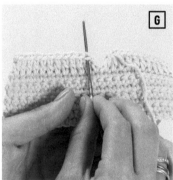

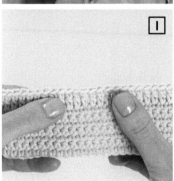

Closing a round with a slip stitch to the top of the starting chain can sometimes create a noticeable seam. Invisible fastening off is therefore a great alternative for projects where a traditional join might be unsightly.

INVISIBLE FASTENING OFF

This method of finishing a round gives an almost seamless finish to your project and is particularly useful for motifs, such as granny squares. This example shows an invisible join made with trebles, but the technique is exactly the same for other stitches, too.

1. When you reach the end of a round, cut the yarn leaving a long tail and draw it through the last stitch, as you would do normally for fastening off.

2. Thread a tapestry needle with the yarn tail and bring it under the top of the 'V' of the first stitch in the round, from front to back (G).

3. Bring the needle back into the last stitch (H) – you'll see this mimics the top 'V' of a finished crochet stitch, and now you can weave in the yarn end (I).

WEAVING IN ENDS

When you've gone to all the trouble of creating a beautiful crochet project, the last thing you want is for it to unravel over time. The best way to prevent this from happening, and to give your projects a longer life, is by making sure your weaving in is top notch.

It's important that when you fasten off your yarn, you leave a good 15cm (6in) tail – this will give you plenty to work with. Cut the yarn and draw this yarn end through the loop on your hook, pulling gently to tighten it close to the stitch. Thread a tapestry or blunt-ended needle with the yarn and, on the wrong side of your crochet, work the needle forwards and backwards a few times through several stitches. Pull the tail slightly before snipping the end away, close to the back of your work – avoiding cutting the stitches at all costs!

TENSION AND MEASURING FOR GAUGE

Tension is a term used to describe how tight or loose your crochet stitches are and varies quite naturally from one crocheter to the next. In order for some patterns to work, particularly wearables, a tension guide or gauge is given at the beginning. This describes how many stitches and rows should fit within a certain measurement, usually 10 x 10cm (4 x 4in).

To make a tension swatch, use the hook size, yarn and stitches stated in the pattern and make a square larger than you need, around 15cm (6in) is ideal. Lay the square flat and use a ruler horizontally to measure the number of stitches in 10cm (4in), beginning at the base of a row to the left of your square. Count how many stitches there are, and repeat on a few other rows to check. Next, use the ruler vertically and count the number of rows in 10cm (4in).

If the number of stitches doesn't match the specified gauge, change your hook size as follows: if the number is too few, try a smaller hook; too many, then a larger one will help.

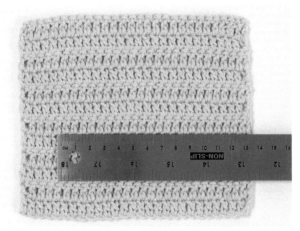

Measuring tension on a sample to count the number of stitches

FINISHING UP

Once you've completed your crochet masterpiece, it's time to add the finishing touches, so fasten off that yarn and weave in your ends (see left) and let's give your project the finish it deserves.

BLOCKING

Blocking is a technique that finishes projects by gently easing them into shape; it helps to define stitches, making them look sharper, and can stop edges from curling, so you can see the intended shape. For garments, it can also relax the stitches and improve the drape.

For all types of blocking, you'll need a suitable surface – a blocking board, cork mats, towels on the carpet or ironing board all work fine – and a set of rust-proof pins.

Before blocking

After blocking

WET BLOCKING

This technique is best suited to yarns composed of mostly natural fibres, but will work for acrylics, too.

Dampen your crochet gently – a spray bottle filled with warm water works well. If your crochet is too wet, don't wring it as you'll stretch the stitches; instead, blot away the excess by pressing the fabric between two towels. Pin out to shape, gently easing it into the dimensions you need, and leave to dry.

STEAM BLOCKING

For synthetic yarns, this method works best as the heat helps to fix the stitches. First, pin out your crochet to shape. Using an iron on the highest steam setting, hover carefully just above your work, pressing the button to release steam evenly over the surface. Make sure you don't touch the yarn with the iron, as you could ruin it. Leave the pieces to cool and dry.

JOINING MOTIFS AND EDGES

If you've made a whole pile of squares for a blanket, or you've got a garment with edges to seam, here are a few of the easiest ways to join them together.

WHIP STITCH

This trusty stitch creates a strong fastening between edges and is virtually invisible. It's perfect for joining multicoloured motifs where a seamless join is preferred.

Place motifs with right sides facing and thread a tapestry needle with a length of yarn that is about two-and-a-half times the length of the edge to join. Beginning at the right edge, join pairs of stitches through the loops furthest away from each other, bringing the needle through the stitches in the same direction each time (A).

This technique can also be used for joining the edges of seams of garments, but join the sides of stitches together rather than the loops.

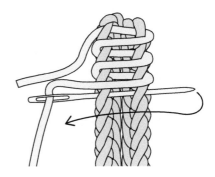

A

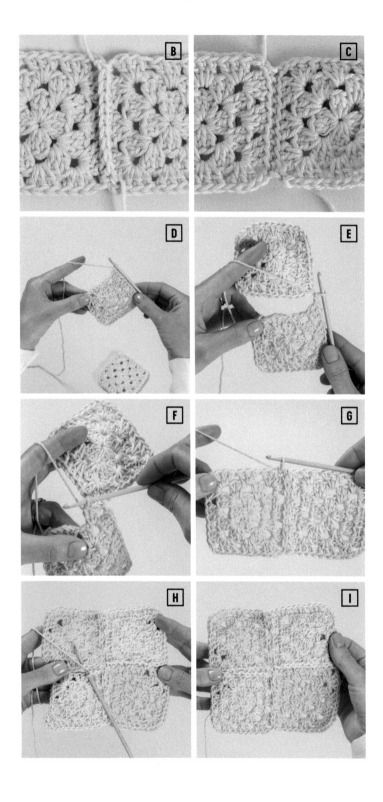

DOUBLE CROCHET SEAM

With some projects, it makes more sense to use your hook to join things together. Double crochet can be used to create a decorative, sturdy seam on the right side of your work when pieces are placed wrong sides together (B). You can get a different effect by hiding the stitches, working with right sides together for seaming, if you prefer (C).

For a double crochet seam, begin at the right-hand edge and join pairs of stitches together through both loops, working double crochet in the usual way (see Basic Stitches: Double Crochet).

JOIN AS YOU GO (JAYG)

This method works well for lots of motif projects and adds the final round to one piece, while at the same time joining it to another. It feels like a good time-saver and helps to progress your project in super-quick time.

This example shows granny squares, but can be adapted for other shapes.

1. First, make one granny square (Square 1) in its entirety and have your next square (Square 2) completed up to the two last sides of the final round.

2. Crochet along the third edge and make the corner cluster, and ch 1 (D).

3. Make a sl st into the corner of Square 1 (E) and complete the corner cluster of Square 2 (F), then *sl st into the next space between clusters of Square 1.

4. Make your next cluster in Square 2; then, rep from * across the side, until you reach the corner of Square 2, make the first cluster here, then sl st into Square 1 as before and complete the corner of Square 2 (G).

5. Repeat the JAYG along the row, joining one square at a time.

6. To begin the next row, join the first square as before along one side. The next square can now be joined on two sides – simply make the square with one side completed before joining exactly as before, but along two sides (H and I).

The first square of any row only joins on one side. All of the following squares will join on two sides.

ACKNOWLEDGEMENTS

This book has been an absolute pleasure to research, design and write, and I could not do it without the help of a seriously awesome team: thanks to the David and Charles gang for asking me to take on this project and having the vision to create such an epic book – to Sarah C for guiding me along the way, to Anna and Sarah R for making it look incredible, to Jason for the great photos (and the coolest music on shoots), and to Carol, Neti and Jane for their impeccable editing skills.

To Annabelle and the Stylecraft team – thank you for the generous yarn support, and to Andrea for her mahoosive yarn balls. To my friends, Chrissie and Sharna, who gave advice and inspiration along the way, and to my bestie Debbie, who thinks I'm a bit bonkers but encourages me, regardless. Lastly to my family for their endless support and love – to my husband, Kevin and my children, Thomas and Annabelle, who are used to living in a house full of yarn.

ABOUT THE AUTHOR

Sarah is a crocheter, designer and author of the award-winning 'Annaboo's House' blog. She taught herself to crochet after giving up teaching following the birth of her second child and began writing a blog as a way of recording her progress. After a few years of crocheting, she now designs patterns for craft and crochet magazines, sells patterns in her Etsy shop, www.etsy.com/uk/shop/AnnaboosHouse and offers free patterns and tutorials on her blog www.annabooshouse.blogspot.com

SUPPLIERS

Stylecraft Yarns www.stylecraft-yarns.co.uk
Woolly Mahoosive www.woollymahoosive.com
Anchor Crafts www.anchorcrafts.com
RICO design www.rico-design.de/en/home
Love Crafts www.lovecrafts.com

INDEX

A DAVID AND CHARLES BOOK
© David and Charles, Ltd 2020

David and Charles is an imprint of David and Charles, Ltd
Suite A, Tourism House, Pynes Hill, Exeter, EX2 5WS

Text and Designs © Sarah Shrimpton 2020
Layout and Photography © David and Charles, Ltd 2020

First published in the UK and USA in 2019

Sarah Shrimpton has asserted her right to be identified as author of this work in accordance with the Copyright, Designs and Patents Act, 1988.

All rights reserved. No part of this publication may be reproduced in any form or by any means, electronic or mechanical, by photocopying, recording or otherwise, without prior permission in writing from the publisher.

Readers are permitted to reproduce any of the patterns or designs in this book for their personal use and without the prior permission of the publisher. However, the designs in this book are copyright and must not be reproduced for resale.

The author and publisher have made every effort to ensure that all the instructions in the book are accurate and safe, and therefore cannot accept liability for any resulting injury, damage or loss to persons or property, however it may arise.

Names of manufacturers and product ranges are provided for the information of readers, with no intention to infringe copyright or trademarks.

A catalogue record for this book is available from the British Library.

ISBN-13: 9781446307502 paperback
ISBN-13: 9781446378793 EPUB

This book has been printed on paper from approved suppliers and made from pulp from sustainable sources.

Printed by CPI Group (UK) Ltd for:
David and Charles, Ltd
Suite A, Tourism House, Pynes Hill, Exeter, EX2 5WS

Publishing Director: Ame Verso
Senior Commissioning Editor: Sarah Callard
Managing Editor: Jeni Hennah
Project Editor: Jane Trollope
Technical Editors: Carol Ibbetson and Neti Love
Proofreader: Claire Coakley
Art Direction: Sarah Rowntree
Designer: Sam Staddon
Photographer: Jason Jenkins
Production Manager: Beverley Richardson
Model: Laura Staddon
Illustrator: Kuo Kang Chen

David and Charles publishes high-quality books on a wide range of subjects.
For more information visit www.davidandcharles.com.

Share your makes with us on social media using #dandcbooks and follow us on Facebook and Instagram by searching for @dandcbooks.

Layout of the digital edition of this book may vary depending on reader hardware and display settings.